Niala Maharaj and Gaston Dorren

THE GAME OF THE ROSE

The Third World in the Global Flower Trade

Published for the Institute for Development Research Amsterdam
by International Books (Utrecht, The Netherlands), 1995

CIP-DATA KONINKLIJKE BIBLIOTHEEK, DEN HAAG

Maharaj, Niala

The game of the rose :
the third World in the global flower trade /
Niala Maharaj & Gaston Dorren. – Utrecht :
International Books. Fig., tab.
Publ. in collab. with INDRA, UvA. With ref.
ISBN 90-6224-981-7
NUGI 661/824
Subject headings: flower trade ; Third World /
development cooperation, business and industry.

Cover design: Tekst/Ontwerp, Amsterdam
Cover photo: Damaris Beems, Amsterdam
Printing: Bariet, Ruinen
Production: Trees Vulto DTP en Boekproduktie, Schalkwijk

Institute for Development Research Amsterdam
Plantage Muidergracht 12, 1018 TV Amsterdam, The Netherlands
tel. 31 (0)20-5255050, fax. 31 (0)20-5255040

International Books
A. Numankade 17, 3572 KP Utrecht, The Netherlands
tel. 31 (0)30-731840, fax. 31 (0)30-733614

Preface

Have you sometimes felt uneasy by the increasing piles of uniform and plastic-looking cut flowers for sale today? In the Netherlands you find them in every second shop and in the many stalls at the corners of streets. Increasingly commercial flowers are becoming a common product in other European countries as well, and the market is now being pushed into the US and Japan. Reading *The game of the rose* I realised that my own uneasy feelings about these flowers did make sense. The book reveals the labour, the capital and the poison behind the rosy picture of flowers – the flowers you buy, you give and receive at every occasion of modern life. If you love rosy pictures don't read *The game of the rose*, for it will change your image of flowers forever.

Flowers are no longer the pure symbols of beauty, wellbeing, celebration, sympathy, respect, or spirituality. Today chrysanthemums, alstroemerias, carnations and roses are big business, they are dangerously polluted markers of the globalisation which holds all of us in its firm grip. *The game of the rose* interconnects the realities of the poorest workers in Africa, Asia, Latin America and Europe – peasant women, children, or illegal migrants – with the main agents of the flows of international capital in the North and the South: the businessmen, bankers, entrepreneurs, middlemen, knowledge producers and consultants who streamline the bio-technology, the production and trade of the cut flowers as long as they benefit from it.

For how long they will remain interested is uncertain, however. The future of this modern cash crop is unpredictable, as flowers are an extremely vulnerable and risky business and the world market in this sector is already showing signs of saturation. This happened before with coffee, tea, coconut, cacao, cotton, sugarcane, jute, rubber and many other agricultural export products introduced to or imposed on the (ex) colonies.

Two to three decades ago, the cut flower market was vastly dominated by the Netherlands. Even today, because of the transnational nature of the flower industry, one out of every five commercially grown cut flowers is produced in the Netherlands, while three out of five flowers crossing international borders have a Dutch passport. But the entire sector of commercial flowers is now built on an intricate set of connections between its Northern and Southern agents, between technology researchers, producers, workers, traders, and consumers all over the world.

Flowers are certainly not a product for small farmers, whether male or female, in developing countries to invest in. It is an extremely fast-paced, capital-intensive and vulnerable product, requiring a high capital, technology and management level. A sudden rise of temperature in Europe with its resulting lower demand for flowers can create a tremendous loss for growers in the South. It is the easy supply of international capital in combination with rock bottom prices for labour which provide the conditions to engage in the flower business. In Columbia peasant women make up 60% of the work force in flower production, earning the lowest income and facing the highest health risks, while many of them are the sole breadwinners of their families.

The empirical data provided in this book were obtained with great difficulty. No research reports were available, and the traders and producers in general did not really enthusiastically react to the idea of revealing the truth behind the rosy picture. Yet the facts brought together leave little doubt that the business elite in the North are the ones to benefit most from the globalised flower industry. In the countries in the South where flower production has eaten away and polluted the land and the water used earlier for food growing, the food prices double every two years. This urges the very poorest to sell their labour for less than the minimum wage, and precisely this vicious circle of exploitation is the basis for this new and 'successful' world trade.

The lowest-paid workers in the flower industry are also the ones whose health is most directly damaged by the high quantities of dangerous pesticides used in the flower industry: headaches, nausea, skin irritation and rash, dizziness, miscarriages, premature and still births, malformations in babies, poisoning of sucklings, asthma, neurological problems, allergies, impaired eyesight and cancers have been reported for instance in Columbia. In the Netherlands, too, the workers are exposed to concentrations of pesticides of up to 60 times the concentration considered to be safe. And what to think of all the environmental consequences, for instance the effects of the amounts of jet fuel used by the air transports to the Northern markets? In the end this will as a boomerang hit back at the Northern hemisphere.

Cut flowers are the latest export crop, creating unhealthy employment at only the lowest wages. It puts food security at risk and destructs land, water and air. The product escapes the ability of governments for monitoring or control, with its infinite room for leakage of foreign exchange, and its sometimes direct connections with the drug scene and the top people in corrupt regimes. There are now extensive tax holidays for entrepreneurs, particularly in countries in Africa. This, together with the predominantly foreign ownership of the flower businesses and the uncertainty of future demand, creates a most questionable basis for developing countries to earn the hard currency dictated by structural adjustment conditions. Yet given the multiple pressures of conventional economic wisdom, debt repayment and the low prices for traditional agricultural export crops, "it is hard to avoid the conclusion that the only path to redemption is through the rose garden", the authors state at the end of their book. This is certainly not the sustainability preached by the development agencies, and therefore, "once you start questioning flower growing, you end up questioning the development model that prepared the ground for it."

As the authors themselves emphasise, this book is a start in a totally new field for research. It raises many questions, for instance from whom and how the land now used for flower growing was obtained, and what happens with this land and the people working in the flower production after entrepreneurs decide to leave the business. There is an urgent need for more indepth research into flowers. The type of knowledge needed refers not merely to the statistics for making cost-benefit analyses, although more of such quantitative data will be most useful. What I have in mind is a deeper understanding of the entire social agency that produces the roses decorating the Dutch, German, North-American and Japanese homes What are the thoughts and practices of the different people embedded in the power dynamics at all levels of the flower business, both in the countries in the South where cut flowers are grown and exported and in the North in the circles of the middlemen and the ranks of the business elite?

Such further research will necessitate the development of methodologies of 'studying-up' – i.e. doing research among the more powerful which is notoriously difficult to do. People in power who are actively involved in capital-intensive, transnational business as a rule have little interest in studies revealing the concrete particulars of their production practices. Yet this is precisely what is needed to unmask the violence of the dominant 'development' model. Further research can show how such 'development' rapidly eats away the possibilities of sustainable wellbeing for all, and how it destructs the lives of people, the earth and the prospects of future generations.

Is that all we can do, helping to unmask the rosy picture of the game of the rose? Books like this one may do more, I feel, they may change the minds of consumers – and in the end, consumers are one of the most powerful pressure groups. One of the practical effects *The game of the rose* at least had on me was, that from now on I will think twice before buying a bunch of flowers. And I will not touch them any longer without good gloves.

January 1995
Joke Schrijvers, Professor of Development Studies,
Institute for Development Research, University of Amsterdam (INDRA)

Table of Contents

CHAPTER I

Introduction

Prejudice. That's how this study began.

'We are helping the Kenyans to grow flowers for export through joint ventures with Dutch companies', a senior development official of the Netherlands remarked in passing some three years ago.

Flowers? was our knee-jerk response. Not food? That's development assistance? We were old-fashioned bigots, we were informed. Flowers brought much-needed foreign exchange to debt-ridden Kenya and used little land. Why should poor people grow food when they could buy it more cheaply from subsidised farmers in Europe using the proceeds from the lucrative flower trade? Import-substitution was an outmoded development strategy. Our fixation with food security identified us as dogmatic dinosaurs.

We retreated in the face of superior economic jargon. But flowers then started springing up everywhere we turned, as History rained destruction on the Cold War era and any questioning of the market solution to Third World poverty. In Ethiopia, as famine continues its cycle. In Colombia, where flowers are meant to be an antidote to the cocaine economy. In structurally-adjusted Zimbabwe, Malawi, Uganda, Ivory Coast, Zaire and numerous other African states. In Brazil, as a debt-swap deal with a German bank, in Costa Rica, Mexico, Ecuador, Peru... And as one prescription for the rehabilitation of the war-veteran economies of Nicaragua, El Salvador, Honduras.

'A group of us started a biotechnology lab to produce food plants', one businessman on a Caribbean island recalled. 'Somehow, when we had got the thing going, it suddenly started producing flower plants. I think the idea came from an Indian consultant we had...'

Our anachronistic doubts about the wisdom of it all refused to lie down and die. Did no-one remember the fate of cut-flowers' ancestors – coffee and tea, those Third World agricultural commodities that had overpopulated the world market after the Second World War only to see their prices dwindle under the weight of bloated supply? Had no-one ever mentioned floriculture's filthy reputation in its home-base, Holland, for being the biggest ecological consumer of all agricultural sectors and the one with the worst – including illegal – labour habits? Was it wise, in this ecocentric era, for developing countries to put savings into a production system that consumes profligate amounts of jet-fuel in getting the product to the market?

Our archaic sentiments were further roused when we discovered that flower-workers in Kenya worked on farms that resembled colonial plantations. Was this a solution to poverty?

As two journalists wishing to investigate the matter further, we were surprised to discover that no-one had done any studies on which we could conduct analysis. The scale of flower-production that we were discovering seemed to suggest that it was the current 'miracle crop' for the Third World. Yet, apart from workers' revelations about conditions on Colombian flower farms, no comprehensive analysis of the sector had been conducted by the economists and statisticians on which we rely for basic information.

Fortunately, a fairy god-mother suddenly turned up. The University of Amsterdam's Institute for Development Research (INDRA) facilitated a small grant from the Fund for University Development Cooperation (FUOS) to conduct preliminary research. We were able to contact businesses, government and non-governmental sources, conduct interviews with responsible officials and actors in the trade and assemble reports and newspaper clippings from Holland, Germany, Britain, Colombia, Zimbabwe, Kenya, India and a few other countries. Unfortunately, our grant was not sufficient to allow us to visit countries in the Third World, so the information contained in this book is lacking in many concrete details.

Our basic aims were: to begin documentation on the scale of the industry, its structure and current effects in developing countries and to attempt an analysis of its potential for helping to solve the structural problems of poverty in the Third World, its likely environmental and socioeconomic consequences and its future effects on the economies of the countries involved.

The resulting report is far less definitive than we would have liked to make it. The first section, on supply, demand and pricing, is quite comprehensive and accurate, and should be useful in formulating any predictions about the future profitability of this trade for developing countries. The second, on the structure of the global trade itself, is also reliable in its details, since we were operating from the main centre of the industry, Holland, and were able to interview numerous insiders and cross-check our information quite thoroughly. But in this first effort to look at the global trends in this sector, thorough investigation of important areas of international financing turned out to be beyond our scope. We simply could not follow all the arcane loops of the international finance system to get the answers we needed. This was largely due to the essential nature of the flower trade itself. Much of the real information is hidden in the accounts of international companies even from governments who may want to understand exactly how much profit is being made in order to levy taxes on it.

In addition, though we have been able to identify the basic patterns of the industry, the information we had at our disposal was a patchwork of testimony from a number of different countries and official and unofficial sources. Since there must be variations between the situations in different regional locations, we have chosen to use key countries to illustrate different aspects of the trade without claiming that these are exactly replicated in the other places.

Thus, for an understanding of the joint ventures between Northern and Southern firms which are an essential element of this sector, the reader needs to read the section on India, where we were most easily able to document this feature. To see where the larger share of the profits go, the section on Kenya is most helpful. The case of Colombia allowed us to provide a picture of workers' conditions, but the key role of current structural adjustment schemes is best illustrated by developments in Zimbabwe. In all of these, the information in incomplete, partly because of the unhelpfulness of official and non-governmental bodies in these countries, and partly because of our own distance from the locus of action. However, we would like to think that, in their totality, our descriptions of the various regions will provide a blue-print of the mechanisms underlying the global system of flower-production.

To the businessmen, bankers, consultants and officials who were very co-operative in our efforts to understand their sector, we must express unqualified gratitude. Often, they were remarkably open and straightforward. Many of these may not agree with our conclusions. But we do wish to make it clear that we do not have anything but respect for them when we draw conclusions that may contradict their own observations about the value of this trade for developing countries. Our role in the world simply demands that we look at the results of their activities with a critical eye.

We would also like to thank Gerda van Roozendaal of the University of Amsterdam's department of International Relations and Public International Law and Frank Brassel and Andrea Quenter of the German non-governmental organisation, FIAN, for sharing the results of their own research with us, and talking through many of the questions that our information raised. In addition, David Slogge, Albert van Oortmerssen, Jochen Hippler, Daniel Nelson and Andrea Leug all supported us with efforts to find documentation in the course of our research.

Finally, we would like to thank the staff at INDRA for their sympathy and understanding throughout this effort, and for the trust they put in two unprofessional researchers in commissioning this book. Though it will not qualify as a rigorous academic study, we hope that it lives up to their expectations of a preliminary investigation into this uncharted territory. We sincerely hope that better qualified researchers will take the issue from where we have left off, and something better will follow.

And that this book will lead to a rethinking of the flower sector among those who have the power to make decisions about agricultural and economic policy in the Third World.

Amsterdam, September 1994
N.M. and G.D.

PART I

The World Flower Sector

CHAPTER 2

The Global Flower Market
Cut Flower Competition

A new War of the Roses is on. Having won the battle over the carnation and after their unsuccessful alstroemeria raid, Third World growers are now out to conquer the rose market. The first skirmishes have ended undecided, since growing demand has absorbed increased production. However, it is only a matter of time before the battle-field is coloured red.

Supply

In the 1960s and 70s, one country rose to overwhelming dominance in the emerging world cut flower trade: the Netherlands. While the Dutch expanded their flower fields from 972 ha in 1960 to 5,697 ha in 1991 – one tenth of the world total – in neighbouring countries, such as Germany, acreage dwindled: from 5,176 ha in 1960 to 2,963 ha in 1988. Production grew even faster than acreage because of ever higher yields.

Today, one out of every five commercially grown cut flowers is produced in Holland, and as much as three out of five cut flowers crossing international borders have a Dutch passport. Few other Western countries have managed to wrestle some share of the international market from the tiny giant on the North Sea: Italy (6 per cent), Israel (4), Spain (2) and France (1).

But a dark horse has galloped up from the South. From the late sixties on, a fast expanding stream of flowers has come from a growing number of Third World countries. Starting from virtually zero, they gained a world market share of about 25 per cent in 1992.[1]

Colombia was the first. Floricultural folklore has it that an American student in the mid-sixties fed lots of possible production sites into his computer, and out came the Bogotá savannah as the ideal location. Since the late sixties, Colombian exports have grown steadily, hitting the 100,000 tons mark in 1991, with a value of 267 million US dollars.

Flowers have become Colombia's fifth biggest legal export item – sixth biggest, all counted. The United States is the main market. However, the European Union has been catching up since it abolished the import duty for Colombian flowers in order to help the country diversify its exports and win the War on Drugs.

The other Third World country that is into flowers in a big way is Kenya. Here, it was a Dane who saw the floricultural potential – and the potential for his numerous black crowns to be put to a respectable use, if a persistent item of gossip is to be given credence. The erstwhile money-launderette developed into the world's largest carnation plantation, Sulmac, and was finally bought by Unilever, again with motives other than plain profit-making (see chapter on Kenya).

In the 1980s, Kenyan output increased almost fourfold as other entrepreneurs followed suit: from 3,788 tons in 1980 to 14,423 tons in 1990. A new growth spurt took place in the early 90s, leading to a record export of 23,635 tons in 1993.[2] Export earnings in the late 80s were in the range of 30 to 40 million US dollars a year[3], which makes flowers one of the country's main foreign currency earners, second only to coffee, tea and tourism. There are about thirty significant companies involved in the industry.

In Asia, Thailand has long held the special niche market for orchids. Starting on a modest scale as early as the fifties, the country flower exports boomed in the mid-eighties and reached an official value of 30 million US dollars in 1991. Estimates including non-registered exports are as high as 80 million dollars. About half is bound for Japan, with Europe and the United States sharing most of the other half.[4]

In each of the three Southern continents, other countries have taken the same road. In Latin America, Peru, Ecuador, Guatemala, Costa Rica, Mexico and Brazil have a well-established export floriculture, the latter two appearing the most ambitious ones. Some Caribbean islands, such as Jamaica, are only just getting involved, as is Chile. In Africa, Zambia, Tanzania, Uganda, Malawi, Mauritius, Ethiopia, Ivory Coast and Morocco have jumped on the bandwagon. In Asia, Malaysia and Taiwan are serious about conquering the Japanese market, as are New Zealand and Australia. Turkey aims at European consumers. Incipient India is in the middle, and might well have a shot at both (see section on India).

World cut flower exports 1992, in 1000s of US$.

Netherlands	2,153,560
Colombia	395,644
Israel	146,120
Italy	111,277
Spain (incl. Canary Islands)	69,086
Thailand	67,579
Kenya	61,477
Zimbabwe	28,743
France	28,162
Ecuador	25,330
New Zealand	18,342
Singapore	18,088
Mexico	17,861
Germany	16,303
Morocco	16,224
USA	14,359
Peru	13,771
Costa Rica	13,531
South Africa	13,377
Turkey	13,290
Australia	12,353
United Kingdom	11,832

Source COLEACP, document distributed at Floriculture Seminar Trinidad & Tobago, 9-10 May 1994, assembled on the basis of European, American and Japanese sources.

Both the number of flower-growing countries and the acreage in several of the established producing countries is rising. Total Southern production is increasing at a rate faster than Northern demand. Apart from trying to force demand up – a course taken by Northern producers, especially Holland – there are two possible consequences: Southern producers may gradually push their Northern competitors off the market and prices may go down. Both things seem to be happening.

Fights over market-shares typically occur over one species at a time.

Carnations were the first battle-ground. Southern producers obviously conquered a very significant market share there, first on the American market, afterwards and to a lesser degree on the European as well. They actually got Northern producers to reduce their acreage significantly.

Then, there was a short-lived alstroemeria riot. Practically overnight, the company Finlay in Kenya planted eleven hectares of it, thereby glutting the market.[5]

'The supply of alstroemeria got out of hand', the Dutch trade magazine remembers with a shudder, 'resulting in a veritable revolt of Dutch alstroemeria growers.'

Prices plummeted, and have not recovered. But the Dutch producers struck back with technological innovations and a wider assortment, and now pride themselves on having warded off the blow.[6]

There is still some alstroemeria-growing in Kenya, but it is nowhere near dominant on the European market. In the opposite hemisphere, Colombia does have a more significant share on the American market.

When the Dutch growers rose in furore over the sudden alstroemeria imports in 1991, there was reportedly a rose-grower attending their meeting. When asked why he was there, he answered:

'We are the next victims, and if we do not take care, we'll go the carnations' way.'

He was right: roses are now what North and South are arm-wrestling over. In both Latin America and Africa, the rose acreage is rising. In the 1994/95 winter season, the African rose supply to the Dutch auctions is expected to grow over a quarter.

The Dutch trade magazine quotes several parties on the strategy to be adopted. One grower suggests that all flowers auctioned should carry a code indicating on what day they were reaped. Since it takes some time to get African and Latin American flowers to the Dutch auction, these are at a disadvantage where freshness is concerned. The date code would 'unmask' them, as the grower put it, and in doing so make them less competitive.

Another grower advocates a kind of floral variety of the Non-Proliferation Treaty on nuclear arms: Dutch companies should not share their – most profitable – knowledge of innovation and new varieties with foreign companies for a couple of years. He seems to forget that the Netherlands, though still dominant as an exporting nation, does not have a monopoly in either growing technology or breeding. Also, the knowledge and the varieties do not rest with the same companies which do the growing, nor are there, generally, all that intimate commercial connections.

Not all parties involved go along with this war-mongering tone. Auctions, breeders, propagators, importers, exporters, all of them take a far more dispassionate position, which can be summarized as, 'Yes, Southern producers will conquer their market share, so let's see how we can still make a profit in that new situation.'[7] What all people involved in the trade point out is that even Northern growers can still make a profit by betting on premium quality, new, fashionable varieties and, to some extent, technologically advanced production methods.

Demand

'It's a business that people are thinking is a golden mountain, but it's not that at all. There will be some increase in demand in the coming years but not as much as people think.'

Jan Lanning,
Senior Consultant for Marketing and Economic Affairs with the Dutch Floricultural Wholesale Board

A trade legend has recently sprouted about the seven 747s full of roses which were unable to quench the unexpected appetite for roses that sprang up in Moscow last Mothers' Day. It has led to wild talk about exploding demand due to the spread of the market economy in Eastern Europe.

Even before that, consultants and advisers to Third World economies were lauding the possibilities of flowers as an export product with a high level of demand in the developed world. They are encouraging Third World farmers to jump into this sector, which has a high return on capital.

'It's a formula for turning soft currency into hard', one of them said to us.

Cut flower imports into the EU, in millions of stems

Roses	1988	1990	1992
Israel	117	135	145
Zimbabwe	5	29	78
Kenya	6	19	66
Morocco	23	38	41
Colombia	15	12	29
Brazil	6	10	18
Ecuador	8	6	17
Zambia	0	4	13
Malawi	0	0	4
other (South)	5	6	7
world total	*241*	*311*	*463*
Carnations			
Colombia	297	385	669
Kenya	156	202	326
Israel	246	213	220
Turkey	27	81	96
Morocco	1	6	27
Peru	1	1	12
Ecuador	1	5	100
other (South)	8	11	9
world total	*1200*	*1277*	*1665*

Note preliminary figures for 1993 indicate a further rise for both roses and carnations.
Source Aalsmeer Nieuws, 18 March 1994, supplement, p. 13. Based on European Union statistical data.

A recent issue of the European Community publication, Courier, carried the following exhortion in bold text:

'Cut flowers and plants are among the most promising products for export from ACP (African, Pacific and Caribbean) countries to the European Union. In 1992, imports into the EU were valued at 604 million ECU, and market growth during the early nineties was 18.2 per cent. During that same period, EU imports from sub-saharan Africa showed a staggering annual growth rate of over 30 per cent, bringing the total annual value of imports from this region from a meagre 28 million ECU in 1980 to over 101 million ECU in 1992.[8]

Such pronouncements sometimes go into the realm of the ridiculous, such as this statement by Herman de Boon of Cebeco Handelsraad Group, a trade cooperative for agricultural products:

'Floriculture products are bought by people. Estimates of the growth of world population show an increase in the number of people worldwide from 5.2 billion now to 6.1 billion in the year 2000 and 10 billion in the year 2050. The increase in the ASEAN countries will be enormous. So, the market size from this point of view is growing.'[9]

Of course, as De Boon admits further on, the only people who can afford to buy flowers are the rich. It is only in the developed world, and among businesses and the elite in poorer countries, that there is a market for flowers. So the growth of demand actually depends on there being a sufficiently large high-income earning sector with the cultural habit of flower buying. In fact, according to a study by the Rabobank in Holland, demand only rose by 11 per cent between 1985 and 1990 in the traditional consuming centres – Europe, North America and Japan. The market increased from 41 to 45 billion guilders then.[10]

The big buyers are in Europe, and they currently consume 50 per cent of global production:

'Dutch people purchase cut flowers and pot plants frequently for use in their own homes', states the Dutch Centre for the Promotion of Imports from Developing Countries (CBI). 'Owing to the low price levels in The Netherlands these purchases are considered to be part of the household shopping and not necessarily luxury items. (...) Because it is a common occurrence in The Netherlands for people to buy flowers for themselves there is a fairly high level of purchasing throughout the year. Special occasions which cause high peaks in expenditure are Mothers Day, Christmas, St Valentine's Day, Easter, birthdays and bereavements.'[11]

This pattern also obtains in Germany and other parts of Northern Europe. The aim is to spread it all over the developed world, particularly in the US and UK, which are relatively low flower consumers. At present, US inhabitants only purchase 14 flowers each year, while the Dutch buy 145. As the Rabobank report states:

'Flowers are luxury products in the US and are bought by only a limited percentage of the population. The buying pattern is very traditional. This can be seen, among other things, from the type of flowers purchased: carnations, roses and chrysanthemums. The more special products are mainly bought by the high earners in the top classes of the population. In all the buyer groups the buying motive is traditional: flowers are mainly bought on special occasions.'

If the flower-marketers are effective, and the recession in the US permits, they will induce a change in cultural habits to their benefit. The bank forecasts that the Japanese market will rise by 5 per cent per year in the coming years, the American by 6 per cent and Europe by 4 per cent. Japan, for instance, is a big user of flowers, but mainly in businesses, so the market has room to grow.

'The custom of buying flowers for one's own use is unknown in Japan', states the Rabobank. 'Because of the growing popularity of the Western lifestyle, this situation is gradually changing. (...) In various countries, floristry products are increasingly seen as products for everyday use and no longer exclusively as a luxury. This shift can be stimulated by better availability and higher efficiency in the business chain, enabling consumer prices to be reduced. (...) In the longer term, when cut flowers become more readily available in greater quantities and purchasing power has increased, Eastern Europe may also develop into an important consumption centre. For the time being, the food supply has priority there.'

But these are hopes. Insiders in this trade are not counting on this kind of speculation.

'Some people say it's more secure to go into the casino than into the flower business', observed Walter Willems, Commercial Manager of the Rijnsburg Flower Auction in an interview. 'No rose grower is talking about the next five years.'

Experienced businessmen can recognise that supply is rising faster than demand. According to the Rabobank, production rose by 12 per cent between 1985 and 1989, which is 1 per cent higher than consumption. In one year alone, 1988-9, production rose by 7 per cent. And those calculations only took into account the largest producing countries.

'Flowers are being overdone', said one veteran flower-marketer from Kenya. 'The market is becoming saturated.'

'There was a time when everything went and everything could be sold', explains Lanning. 'But things have been pretty bad in the last number of years. There are no guarantees in this business.'

A key factor for Third World producers is the seasonability of demand. Flowers are largely required from tropical countries during the winter months in Europe, when production costs there shoot up. During summer, local producers can fulfil the lower demand caused by the neglect of indoor decor.

'When women are naked [on the beach], the trade is dead', is a well-known saying in the Dutch flower trade.

The CBI publication states: 'Imports are most important in the winter months from October-November until April-May. From May onwards the trade is supplied largely by Dutch growers.'

Interestingly, this seasonal demand is reflected in the taxes levied on flowers entering the European community from outside. Between November and May, the tariff is 15 per cent, but from June to October it goes up to 20. ACP (African, Caribbean and Pacific) countries are excused from paying this tariff, which makes the trade a profitable one for them. This status is also applied to some countries in Latin America, such as Colombia.

Prices

This is how the Dutch trade journal comments on price developments in 1993:

The stories behind the prices in 1993

Prices for standard carnations have picked up slightly after a dramatic decrease in 1991. Imported produce fetched a much lower price. Dutch growers are recommended to go for either top quality in bulk varieties or special varieties, such as fancy colours.

Prices for spray carnations have risen, thanks to lower supply from Mediterranean countries. Dutch ones get a 10 per cent higher price than total average (29 compared to 26.5 cents). Kenya has reduced its spray carnation acreage. Price level in spray carnations is strongly Influenced by weather in Holland and import volume.

The alstroemeria price has gone down and will remain at this low level, maybe decrease even a little more. Imported flowers are even worse off, suffering a stronger price drop. The low price is due to both import growth and, particularly, increase in domestic supply brought about by favourable weather conditions and technical improvements.

All types of roses got better prices in 1993, and prices have generally been going up since 1989. In the large- and small-bloom types there is strong international competition. Dutch growers trust their quality will save their share. In spray roses, the price rise has benefitted African growers most. Expectations for 1994 are also positive. Spray roses are labour-intensive, therefore Dutch growers are not too keen on expanding their acreage.[12]

However, oversupply of roses will soon push prices down. 'The problems in the rose sector are still to come. Nearly everyone is convinced that they will come. (...) In the last season, African rose supply [to Dutch auctions] doubled and in the coming season this rise may be no less. Just when the problems of oversupply will make themselves felt, to what degree and for how long are questions nobody dares comment on. (...) But it is really a miracle that this season had a happy ending, so it is said.'[13]

In spite of this, experts from the North encourage developing countries to think that the flower market has a rosy future. As a Zimbabwean newspaper put it in 1992,

'The overproduction and oversupply of horticultural produce on the international market does not pose a threat to Zimbabwe because the country produces high-quality products', the chief executive of the Horticultural Promotional Council, Mr John Logan, has said. As more countries turn to horticultural production, with the majority going into roses, markets overseas are overflowing, suppressing prices.

'At last week's international floriculture seminar in Harare, experts urged Africa to expand its horticultural crops, currently dominated by roses, and improve the quality of its produce, if it is to maintain a foothold on the international market.

"We have quite a good reputation for quality. (...) (Over-production and over-supply) are not a threat to us"', Mr Logan said.[14]

A veteran banker who has been involved in funding such projects in Zimbabwe was far less sanguine in his comments to us.

'They do it too fast', observed Martin de Jong of the Dutch Development Bank (FMO), which no longer entertains applications for loans in this sector outside Zimbabwe where it has a firm stake in one enterprise. 'I am convinced that at least a quarter of the growers in Zimbabwe are making a loss.'

But the prices of all flowers are not falling. The lower prices largely apply to what are called mass flowers, and those are the main ones that are produced in the Third World.

'The prices at which cut flowers are sold at the Dutch auctions are indicative of the international price trend for those products', states the CBI booklet. 'In spite of the sharp rise in supply the average nominal price of cut flowers remained virtually constant over the last ten years. Average nominal prices of the most frequently sold flowers have, however, fallen, indicating that increased supply is making some mass products less profitable. Between 1991 and 1992 average flower prices at Dutch auctions fell by 6.5 per cent. The average price of a stem in 1992 was 38 cents.'

Apart from over-supply of 'mass flowers' (carnations, chrysanthemums), there are a couple of other factors which put the Third World growers at a disadvantage. According to one trader from Kenya, the flowers that are flown in from abroad are always given a lower price, since they are perceived to be less fresh and are expected to last for a shorter time.

'For both cut flowers and pot plants, lasting quality and freshness are the most important requirements in making a purchase. Dutch people always look for "good value for money", and, given that they buy flowers and plants mainly for themselves, these must last as long as possible.'

Prices for Dutch flowers were fairly good in 1993. The gap with prices for imported flowers, which have always been lower, widened. The explanation for this is the difference in quality. Growers' organizations, auctions, the Promotion Bureau and the Production Board for Ornamental Plants have been alarming the growers into improving their quality so as to beat off the competition. These efforts are now starting to pay off, if not in all species. In spite of this, profit margins for Dutch growers are under pressure due to several factors.[15]

Many people see a drop in prices as not necessarily a bad thing for the industry.

'A price reduction need not necessarily imply a cut in producer prices', the Rabobank observes. 'It can also be achieved by removing import barriers and redistributing the margins in the chain.' (...) On average, consumers in Italy, Norway and Switzerland spend a great deal of money on cut flowers. Because of the high price, the number of units that can be purchased for the amount spent is low. In view of the world demand curve it may be expected that if prices were to be halved in those countries, the quantities sold could virtually double."[16]

If you are involved in the trade in flowers rather than the production of them, higher sales volumes, despite lower prices, may make your business increasingly profitable.

'The philosophy in Holland now is to leave production to the overseas guys', Han van den Meerendonk, a consultant with the Dutch Royal Tropical Institute said to us, 'But make sure that breeding stays in your own hands.'

That is an overstatement. Certainly a large part of the production of flowers still remains in Northern countries. However, these are increasingly the more high-value flowers, the ones with novelty value. But the entire trade in this increasingly globalised sector remains almost totally in the North. And that is where profits are really high. As we will see in the following chapter.

CHAPTER 3

The Trade
Plant Money – Reap Flowers

When you buy a flower, you think you are paying for a part of the natural world, an object that represents its unpredictability, mortality, spontaneous beauty. Today, though, what you actually get is an industrial product. The commercial flower's jet-setting life is one of rigid control and regulation, often by computers. Its conception takes place in the sterile world of biotechnology; its colour and shape is designed by fashion-experts and the marketing world. It often feeds totally on chemicals, inhabits soil which has been made biologically dead and is protected from nature by plastic and glass coverings, toxic substances and a precisely controlled system of heating and cooling.

All of these different processes are dictated by humans, who make a profit out of them. The growing process only earns an estimated 10 per cent of the final price of this consumer product. The rest goes to air transportation companies, refrigerated trucking firms, the makers of chemical inputs, the high-tech breeders of the species, the marketing experts, consultants, traders and other middlemen who are indispensable to this intensely modern business.

The key: capital

According to all accounts, modern commercial flower-growing is a particularly capital-intensive sector. In other words, if you want to make money, what you plant is money. It doesn't matter where you do this. The key, stress all experts in this business, is access to the knowledge and technology developed in the North, particularly in Holland and Israel. In this context, technology does not mean machinery as much as chemicals and management systems. For it is the use of these factors, according to all insiders, which marks off the profitable commercial flower-grower from his less-successful competitor. First, the soil is fumigated with the ozone-destroying gas, methyl bromide (forbidden now in some Northern countries), which leaves it biologically dead. Then high-tech species developed in the labs and breeding grounds of the North are planted according to a meticulously designed system, again developed in the North. They are fed chemicals according to a precise programme, then harvested at just the right moment, then cooled to a precise temperature, then flown to the market.

The North-South divide: knowledge, technology and labour

That technology can be shifted to the Third World, where it can be combined with the cheap labour that is the hallmark of 'developing' countries, and yield as high, or higher, returns on investment. With the development of air transportation and environmental awareness in the last two decades, such a system of organisation became increasingly feasible and desirable. Flower-growing is notorious as an environmental polluter and consumer of resources in Holland. Even before environmental groups began to accuse the Dutch growers of being some of the biggest polluters of that country, joint ventures began to develop so as to shift some of the production to Africa and other parts of the Third World. The low cost of labour there turned out to be a major boon. But the consumers are in the North, and so are those who know them – the marketing experts. So the sector is now built on an intricate set of linkages between its Northern and Southern elements, between the technology producers, growers, traders and sellers.

'Knowledge' is usually given a higher value in modern times than labour. Thus, for those involved in the flower industry, it is quite understandable that 'market experts' in the North should be paid more than labourers in the South. The whole business is founded on the essential schism between the value put on human work in North and South, and its structure perpetuates this. Retailers, who put a 100 per cent mark-up on the prices of the flowers they buy, cite the high cost of making bouquets as one reason. It takes fifteen minutes to put a bunch of flowers together in a way that conforms with the aesthetic values of Northern people, it seems. Of course, each of those flowers may have demanded more than fifteen minutes of workers' time in the growing process back in Africa or Latin America. But that time is given a lower money value. It is bound up with assembly-line-type mass production – routine activity. The managers of the flower-factories in Africa and Latin America, who are usually foreign, are the ones who have the skills. And so do the flower-arrangers in the shops, and the breeders who design the flowers in the first place.

Still a fragile business

Despite the intense modernity of the sector, however, the fragility of the product still remains. Thus, a consignment of flowers may leave the farm in excellent condition and yet be valueless when it arrives at the airport, due to insufficient cooling. It may leave the airport in pristine condition, but a delay in flight times, or an unscheduled stop-over may make it valueless once it reaches the market. Hence, flower-producers in the Third World have to keep their costs extremely low to compensate for these factors. Rock-bottom prices for labour are one mechanism for doing this.

The globalisation of the trade intensifies the vulnerability of flower-production. A sudden rise in temperatures in Europe can mean lower demand, as consumers pour out of their homes to enjoy the good weather, and production soars in the North due to the increased daylight and reduction in costs as growers there achieve high yields. This amounts to tremendous loss for growers in the South. At the same time, unexpected shifts in weather conditions in the South can lose millions of dollars in destroyed produce.

And this inherent vulnerability of the product makes the flower-trade a particularly fast-paced one, where large sums of money can be made or lost in the twinkling of an eye. A good symbol of this is provided by the large electronic clocks in the flower auction rooms in Holland. According to all accounts, 'the clock', as it is fondly referred to by veterans, is the central mechanism which sets the current average world price for any particular variety of flower, since a large percentage of global produce passes before it. In these auction rooms, bunches of flowers move by conveyor belt through two hatches at the front, while their source, condition and species is described by an auction official over a loudspeaker. As they pass, the price on the clock falls steadily till one of the buyers in the room presses a button to indicate that s/he is willing to pay the current price on the dial for the consignment of blooms. This is the origin of the cultural concept in English known as the Dutch auction. But for the flower industry itself, the mechanism illustrates the quick reflexes that are an inherent part of the game.

And the scene in the auction room further illustrates the perpetual movement that is an inherent feature of the commercial flower's life. When it is not on a cooled truck dashing to an airport somewhere in the East of Africa, it is on a plane to the wholesalers, or on another plane or temperature-controlled vehicle heading from the wholesale centres to some distant part of Europe or the Middle East, or even Japan. Even when it is being inspected for sale, it is on the move through the auction room by conveyer belt.

In addition, demand is also highly volatile. For, according to all insiders, fashion is the key element. As we all know, fashion is a fickle master, its main principle being novelty. To invest in a crop which is out of step with its latest mass whim can mean having to dump your entire product. If you don't keep your eye glued to the market in this fast-moving business, if you are not in touch with the buyers in the North, you're dead meat. And fashion, in this trade, also means keeping up with the events and seasons, regular and irregular, in the centres of consumption. Besides Christmas, Easter, Valentine's Day, which can be catered for on the annual calendar of the Third World producer by scheduling production to produce red-and-white blooms, then white ones, then masses of red roses, there are the one-off events that demand unusual colours. During the World Cup competition in 1994, for instance, there arose a thirst for orange blooms in Holland, orange being the colour of the national soccer team. This means Southern producers are always at a disadvantage.

The supremacy of marketing

Everyone in the industry stresses that the flower sector is a highly market-driven one. Every piece of trade literature repeats this. Since the sector is aimed at fulfilling a very vague and sentimental 'need', demand is subject to infinite manipulation. The Flower Council of Holland alone spends 30 million guilders per year on promoting the buying of 'Dutch' flowers, which includes those which are exported from Holland but originate in the developing world. The council fosters such new cultural concepts as 'Grandparents' Day' and 'Thank You Day', to encourage the purchase of flowers. Suppliers from developing countries must contribute 1.5 per cent of the price they get to the Dutch auctions towards advertising costs.

Thus, it is the current consumerist culture which determines the growers' activities, not the other way around. Flowers are not simply grown and offered on the market. The market is analysed, pushed, pulled and manipulated first – and then the grower is instructed what to grow and how to grow it. The flower-growers in the outposts of the Third World, therefore, must use the services of expensive 'market-experts' in the North. They are highly dependent on the 'information services' sold to them by consultants, agents and traders. Everyone interviewed for this book stressed that this is a highly knowledge-intensive industry. By this, the meant not just the knowledge of breeding and growing commercial flowers, but selection of types that suit the market. Some small players in the Caribbean islands, for instance, used to bank on production of indigenous species such as heliconias and anthuriums which are easy for them to grow. But the market for these has turned out to be limited. If they are serious about this business, a European consultant told them at seminars in 1994, they need to expand into the segment of the trade where there is real mass demand – roses, carnations and so on.

The design of the product

A marketable flower is nothing like the one you grow in your garden. Longevity is of prime importance when a bloom has to spend one day in cold storage, possibly two or three in transportation and then a couple of others in the shop before it gets into the hands of the consumer. From the point when it is picked, therefore, it must be able to hold out for two weeks. It cannot have too narrow stems, or it will be too fragile for transportation, but it cannot be too heavy either, or it will cost too much in air freight.

And then, there is the other complication: looks. The durable flower also has to be of 'even quality', that is, it must look exactly like the others in the consignment so it can be classified and graded when it enters the sales arena. To guarantee this standardisation, plantlets with a genetic pedigree make for the most sensible course. Moreover, the commercial breeders, who keep a close eye on the market, can supply unusual species which make your product stand out from the others in the flower-shop and cater to the consumers' need for novelty.

Extract from publicity material of a florigenetics firm

Florigene's main field of activity is changing the flower colour of chrysanthemum, carnation, rose, gerbera and lily. These traits have been selected because biochemically and genetically much is already known about the synthesis of flower colours. Furthermore, much attention is given to resistances and tolerances. Florigene's second aim is to incorporate resistances to diseases and insects into existing or new commercial varieties.

A great advantage of biotechnology is that a perfect variety – in terms of cultivation, flower induction, stem length, flower yield, etcetera – can be changed whilst preserving all the other desired characteristics. In this way a breeder can present a totally new range of varieties while keeping yield and other plant characteristics uniform.

This is why breeders and bio-technologists get so much of the profit of the current industry. They have to be paid royalties on each plant of the species they have spent years developing (60 cents on every 1.20 US dollar rose plant cultivated in Kenya, for instance). Again, this is a capital-intensive and knowledge-intensive part of the chain of production, and it takes place in the North. Apart from extensive cross-breeding, they introduce genes into plants to produce different colours, extend vase-life and create new varieties.

The life-cycle of each of their cultivars is getting shorter and shorter, as, in this competitive world, there is increasing demand for novelty. This is one of the reasons, many people in the trade say, there is no hope for small producers in the Third World. They simply cannot afford the latest varieties which produce the big profits, and even if they can, propagators will not trust them to pay the royalties owed to the breeders. They are always behind the market. Even the large producers are always at a disadvantage, for they receive the latest species two years after they have been developed. And these have to be further tested to suit growing conditions in warmer climates.

Government assistance

To enable their firms to make the most of their traditional advantage in knowledge and technology, European governments habitually offer taxpayers' money to industrial and agricultural sectors which generate national income. In the case of the flower sector, the Dutch government has recognised that it is an area in which this country has a lead which should be maintained through technological development. Hence, grants and subsidies are available for companies conducting research into such areas as biotechnology, development of new species, development of installations for the mechanisation of processes, environmental protection and energy conservation measures. It is possible to get grants from the Dutch government, stated Dr. J.W. Vriethoff of BNS Consultants during an interview, of up to 40 per cent for technological development and 50-60 per cent for research. In addition, further grants are available from European Community funds. Both small and large companies are eligible, but it is easier for bigger companies because their research plans tend to be more ambitious. Individual grants usually range from 2-300,000 Dutch guilders, but bigger projects can get one million.

The producers

Again, in this aspect of the chain of production, capital is the key element. The systems of production which produce the kind of even quality that can compete on the international market demand a high level of inputs, mainly produced in the developed world. (See sections on Kenya, Zimbabwe and Colombia.) Huge amounts of chemicals – fertilisers, pesticides, preservatives – are used preventively to guarantee the kind of flawless bloom that is demanded by the Northern consumer. There must be no hint that bugs, or excessive rainfall or sunshine was part of this flower's experience. Thus, protective covering is often used, and irrigation systems, and even heating.

All of this requires money. And so do the transportation, sorting and cooling systems that are necessary to get the flowers in optimum condition to the distant market. Thus, the owners of flower farms must be either foreigners investing in the developing world, governments, or members of the local elite. Very often the managers and plant experts are hired from outside, usually from Holland and Israel. These are paid very high salaries because of their expertise, in the case of Columbia, reportedly, up to 200,000 dollars per year.

For the workers, flower-production is not much different from shoe-production, or any other kind of industrial work. They just have to follow instructions provided by management. Payment and working conditions are also similar to those of other large-scale industry where production sites have shifted to poorer regions. Details of this are dealt with in the sections of this book which describe conditions in Colombia and Kenya.

The middlemen

Apart from the very large growers, most Third World producers must channel their flowers through an importer in one of the consuming countries. These firms take a cut of between 6 and 10 per cent of the wholesale price earned. Often they take flowers on consignment, i.e., if the flowers are not sold, then they pay nothing to the grower. In their hands, too, is the determination of whether, or how much of, the consignment has arrived in good enough shape to be sold on the international market. These firms vary in size. East African Flowers, for example, handles about 600 million stems from Kenya each year, and 20 million each from Tanzania, Uganda and Malawi. The power of this company in relation to this sector in some of those countries is reflected in the fact that East African Flowers handles 80 per cent of the produce of Tanzania and 50 per cent of that of Uganda. The company is growing, according to its head, Simon van der Burg, at a rate of 20 per cent per year.

The largest middlemen of all are the Dutch auctions. They began as co-operatives of flower-growers in Holland and formally still have that structure, but they have been growing rapidly and are now businesses in their own right. Of all roses imported into the European Community in

1992, 50 per cent went through Holland, 40 per cent through the auction and 10 per cent through other traders; in carnations, the total figure is 42 per cent, 29 through the auctions and 13 through the traders. Their sales of cut flowers in 1993 amounted to 3.7 billion Dutch guilders. Of this, half a billion guilders' worth, or 14 per cent, came from the developing world. Foreign growers must pay around 8 per cent in commissions and handling fees to the auctions, a higher rate than auction members, who pay 5 per cent.

To get an appreciation of the scale of this middle layer of the trade, see the accompanying box which reproduces a section from the publicity material of one of the Dutch auctions, the Bloemenveiling Aalsmeer. Profits of this auction alone were 17 million Dutch guilders in 1993.

Extracts from publicity leaflet of one Dutch auction

Bloemenveiling Aalsmeer may rightfully call itself the largest flower auction in the world. Moreover, the term 'largest' can be used in several senses. First of all, the auction building is the largest in the world: a complex of halls measuring approx. 710,000 square metres, which contains 13 electronic auction clocks...

As regards supply and turnover, Bloemenveiling Aalsmeer is also the largest auction in the world. Each day, nearly 16 million flowers and more than 1.7 million plants, representing hundreds of varieties, are auctioned here. In 1993, a total of more than 4.5 billion cut flowers and approx 453 million plants found their way to customers in the Netherlands and abroad. Eighty per cent of the auctioned products were sold abroad by exporters.

1993 turnover Dfl. 2.3 billion
The 1993 turnover of Bloemenveiling Aalsmeer amounted to 2.3 Dutch guilders, more than nine times the turnover achieved in 1972 (250 million guilders). Of the 1993 turnover, cut flowers accounted for 1.5 billion guilders. Dutch products comprise the majority share of this turnover, supplemented by production from abroad. Cut flower imports in 1993 amounted to more than 236 million guilders.

Since Bloemenveiling Aalsmeer, being a cooperative, is a non-profit organisation, it attempts to keep the auction percentage for its members as low as possible. In 1994 the commission percentage, that has remained almost constant since 1972, is 5 per cent, plus a levy on each batch and trolley...

Many major exporters have chosen the flower auction in Aalsmeer for their premises. The products they buy through the auction rooms are prepared for export on site... Including the estimate for export packaging, horticultural products worth a total of 3.5 billion guilders leave the BVA complex for destinations abroad each year.

Use of the building
Some 350 exporters and wholesalers of flowers and plants have their premises in the building. For the export to proceed quickly and efficiently, the building also accommodates a dispatch and loading centre, transport companies, forwarders, KLM Cargo, the Plant Protection Service and the Customs. The auction complex also houses the Cultra Wholesale centre, where retailers can buy a wide variety of horticultural products. In addition, there are offices used by consulting agencies, the Commodity Board and bookkeeping firms.

Branches of the leading merchant banks and various restaurants complete the services to the 1,700-odd companies enrolled as buyers of plants and flowers. All in all, Bloemenveiling Aalsmeer and the other firms occupying space in the auction building provide employment for about 10,000 people.

Re-export – a profitable business

From the wholesale auction-rooms, the flowers again begin to cross national borders to reach their eventual consumers. Some of the importers who first brought them out of the Third World are also exporters and include transport and other elements of the whole chain into their operations. The publicity material reproduced here demonstrates the highly modernised, capital-intensive nature of this part of the trade.

Extracts from publicity leaflet of one import-export company

'Zurel is an experienced importer and exporter of cut flowers and potted plants. With offices in all of Holland's flower auctions, the company also maintains sales offices in Spain, France and the US. In addition, Zurel has established subsidiaries and joint ventures in a number of other countries, currently employs some 600 personnel world-wide and, in 1991, had an annual turnover amounting to more than 250 million dollars. Zurel imports flowers and plants from more than 40 different countries, with exports reaching another 60 nations. The latter account for approximately 80 per cent of the company's activities.

Processing an average of 3 million stems a day, close attention to the logistical aspects is required. Each box of flowers receives an individual bar-code before being automatically weighed and forwarded to the company's expedition department for eventual truck or air transport. The internal transport of the goods is carried out by a conveyor belt, which is equipped with a laser capable of reading the information contained in the bar-codes. The laser is, in turn, connected to Zurel's central computer, thus enabling the location and status of each shipment to be determined at any time. This system also greatly facilitates the preparation of export documents.

Zurel began investing in automation in the mid-1970s, and all aspects of the company's logistical processes are now handled by computer. When a sales-person receives an order, it is entered directly into the computer, thus making the information immediately accessible to anyone who may need it. Zurel's computer department, which operates 24-hours-a-day, currently employs some 20 people. This around-the-clock service is necessary in order to cover time differences in the relay of data via satellite from Zurel's foreign sales offices, sales personnel and clients.

Within Europe, Zurel supplies its customers via temperature-controlled trucks, which ensures that transportation can take place regardless of the weather conditions...'

The retailers

This section of the trade puts a mark up of up to 100 per cent on the product in Europe and as much as 300 per cent in North America.

CHAPTER 4

Transport
Flights of Flowers

One 35-ton cargo plane needs to leave Colombia every three hours to fly that country's flowers to their overseas consumers. It joins the scores of others crisscrossing the globe loaded with roses, carnations, orchids and other blooms. Many of these must be chartered for the purpose, since there is not enough regular air traffic to and from poor countries, especially in Africa, to justify normal flights. Just one Dutch importing company, East African Flowers, has to charter twelve Boeing 707s for flights from Nairobi to Amsterdam each week.

The Third World flower boom has therefore created a lucrative new market for air freight companies, forwarders and airlines. Between one-third and one-half of the wholesale price of Third World flowers goes to pay air freight costs. René W. Barbe, General Manager of the firm Visbeen International Air Services, showed us one bill for a consignment of flowers which left Columbia valued at 2,900 dollars and whose freight cost to Amsterdam was 2,230 dollars. And once the cargo has arrived in Europe or the United States, it is still a long way to the vase. Sometimes, this distance is also covered by aeroplane, as in the notorious case of flowers flown from Nairobi to Amsterdam, auctioned in nearby Aalsmeer and then flown on to Tokyo or New York. More typically, however, from Amsterdam, Frankfurt or London they are trucked to retailers in the same or a neighbouring country. All of these different phases of transportation incur high costs and high headache-levels for the growers.

'At the moment of harvesting, the quality [of African cut flowers] is in most cases better than in Holland', the Dutch trade journal, Vlakblad voor the Bloemisterij, stated. 'Loss of quality takes place between harvesting and auctioning.'[17]

That is, in transport.

Problems are manifold. Roads between farms and airport tend to be bumpy, rendering every truck-journey adventurous and risky.

'We don't have coolers on the lorries', a flower grower from Kenya said at a floricultural seminar in Harare in 1992, 'because they used to fall off, due to the road conditions'.

This was not the complaint of some inept, marginal producer; it was a representative of Sulmac, the number one flower grower in Kenya and probably the biggest carnation farm in the world, the sort of company that can afford to have the road improved and the coolers reinstalled, as indeed the same representative added Sulmac was about to do. But it is easy to imagine the transport problems smaller growers in Kenya and in countries with less infrastructure face.

At the airport, bad handling or lack of cool storage capacity is sufficient to cause the flowers to go to waste. And then there is the persistent fear of flying.

The air freight bottleneck

'Over a long period of time, inadequate air cargo capacity has been the major limiting factor to horticultural exports', L.W. Waithaka of the Kenyan Horticultural Crops Development Authority said at the Nairobi seminar in 1994.

It is a complaint that riddles the literature on Third World flower production. It exploded into a long-running three-way battle in the Zimbabwean press in the late eighties between the national airline, Affretair, local growers and the Dutch national airline, KLM, that ended with both the governments of Zimbabwe and Holland and the editorialists of Zimbabwean newspapers getting involved.

For the flower-growers in the South, the freight costs of the established airlines are very expensive. The trade makes little economic sense to these airlines, since there is a demand for cargo space going in one direction, but not on the return trip. Local airlines, such as Zimbabwe's Affretair, have immense difficulties fulfilling the needs of the exporters, and their rates have to be high.

The giant Southern flower-planters such as Kenya's Sulmac and Oserian have long been making their own arrangements so they do not have to depend on the commercial companies. Sulmac charters five planes per week from the company, German Cargo, to take its produce to the wholesale sectors. But for the smaller producers, availability of freight space is always a problem, especially during the winter when huge amounts of produce have to be rushed from the South to take advantage of the sharp increase in demand. In Kenya, the competition for cargo space becomes a dog-eat-dog struggle at times. Produce from small farmers is often left behind when cargo space is at a premium. They don't have the local muscle of their middle-sized competitors.

And in general, this structural problem of the trade puts an upward pressure on air fares. It also allows carriers to be choosy as to what cargo they like best. Cargo with a high weight per volume is more profitable for them than light things such as flowers. Already Thai orchid growers face higher prices than they were accustomed to because Royal Thai Airlines prefers fruits for its flights to Europe and computer parts for those to California. In 1991, only 70 per cent of foreign orders could be fulfilled for lack of air freight capacity, Thai exporters complained.[18]

This is where the charter-agents such as East African Flowers have stepped in, cutting deals with any outfit who have planes to rent at cheap rates. According to the head of the company, Simon van der Burg, they get planes from African companies such as Angolan Airways and Nigerian Airways. Having such a haphazard, adventurous factor as a structural component within such a fast-paced business introduces other realms of uncertainty. As a Dutch grower in Zimbabwe, Cees Rademaker, recounts:

'We once lost a good number of roses because our pilot ran out of fuel in Nigeria. He landed there on the weekend and had to wait for fuel for two days. So we could forget about those roses.'[19]

International florilore is full of similar tales. As one consultant pointed out, the planes that are available for charter are often old and rickety.

'Well', Simon van der Burg agreed, 'the 707s we charter are not the youngest. 707s haven't been built for twenty years, you know'.

With this business, the company has been growing at a rate of 20 per cent per year. Since it provides transport for 40 growers and does marketing for 15 of them, its total cost to some growers is 50 per cent of the wholesale price. These are still cheap prices, and the profit margins of growers in distant lands depends on their remaining cheap.

Air freight for flowers in US$ per kilo

To Miami, Florida (17 December 1990)

From	Colombia	0.83-1.00
	Ecuador	0.83-0.85
	Peru	0.90
	Jamaica	0.28
	Mexico	0.57
	Thailand	3.97

To Frankfurt, Germany (21 January 1991)

From	Colombia	2.35-2.70
	Kenya	2.27
	Morocco	1.08
	Thailand	4.09-5.55

These figures apply to cargo-only planes or loads over 500 kilo carried by passenger planes. Smaller amounts are more expensive.

Very roughly, one kilo of flowers is equivalent to 25 stems. Allowing for packaging, a ton amounts to some 24,000 stems. Large-bloom roses, the sort most exported by Colombia, are almost double that weight, so half the number of pieces to the ton. Small-bloom roses, the type most exported from Africa, are lighter, so that a ton may comprise as much as 35,000 stems.

Source   Deutscher Gartenbau, 1992, issue 22, p. 1377.

However, this cannot be guaranteed beyond the shortest term. Several types of cheap old aircraft are being phased out because of their high pollution and noise levels and will no longer be allowed to land in European airports in eight years' time (2002). This will mainly affect the African growers. According to Frits Bisschop, Cargo Director of Amsterdam airport, African exporters are already shifting to 747s. These are also quite noisy and dirty, but will be allowed to roar and pollute into the 21st century.

Exporters in Thailand and other East Asian countries, such as Malaysia and Singapore, expect air freight capacity to become even scarcer in the late nineties. The rise in demand for passenger planes is so strong that aircraft manufacturers are not capable of building sufficient cargo planes at the same time.[20] Air freight costs also depend heavily on two factors which are among the most unpredictable in the whole economic realm: the exchange rate of the American dollar (a beacon in the rough sea of economic life – and therefore going up and down like a yoyo) and that of crude oil. When the Gulf War sent oil prices up, flower exporters based far from the main markets ran into trouble. Between November 1990 and January 1991, Colombian exporters were faced with a 45 per cent hike in air fares to Europe.

And it is increasingly becoming recognised that getting the flowers to the customers is a highly energy-consuming affair. For instance, flying 44 tons from Southern Africa to Western Europe consumes 60 tons of jet fuel. Adding the energy consumption of trucking the flowers from the farm to the airport and from the airport to the customer, it is safe to say that a vase holding a bunch of ten imported flowers, with a weight of about 400 grams, contains not only a liter of water, but also well over half a liter of oil.

This is currently being alluded to in the efforts of Dutch growers to stave off the competition from the South. A recent report in the influential Dutch daily, de Volkskrant[21], which analysed the prospects for more eco-friendly horticulture in North and South, included the transport factor in the calculations of environmentally damaging consequences of this trade. It is likely that this will increasingly be the trend in the debates of the future.

Major environmental groups are pressing for value added tax to be levied on jet fuel, as is normal practice with other fuels. An Economic Union plan to green-tax all major energy sources, including oil and natural gas, was stopped by a minority of member states, but is still lurking in Brussels desk drawers waiting to be revived.

On the other hand, this will also effect Northern growers, since they are major consumers of natural gas. According to the same Volkskrant article, the Dutch Agricultural Economic Institute has calculated total energy use of Dutch and African growers to be comparable: 6 to 7 Dutch cents per rose.

Also, against all the threats to Third World growers' profitability, there is the hope of transport by container ship, which consumes less energy. Improving container technology may make this possible some time soon. Already there are regular services between Central America and Florida.

CHAPTER 5

Development Assistance
The Making of a Boom

Since the flower sector is primarily in the hands of the private sector and often involves international capital, it seems that most of the facilitation of the trade is done, not through direct grants from international financing institutions or foreign governments, but via the creation of promotional conditions.

Trade incentives

A major spur to the development of the flower industry in the Third World has been the absence of tariffs on European imports of flowers from African, Caribbean and Pacific nations. Compared to other Third World countries whose products are subjected to a levy of up to 20 per cent when they enter the European market, these 'less-developed countries' have an advantage. This is a part of the Lomé package of assistance measures. Around 1990, the same advantage was extended to some Latin American countries, notably Colombia, Peru and Ecuador, for the same reason. The aim was to reduce those countries' dependence on cocaine as a source of export revenues. The result was a dramatic rise in flower-exports from Colombia. Thus, this forfeiting of customs duties on the part of the rich EU acts as an effective financial contribution towards the development of the industry in poor countries.

Structural adjustment

Structural adjustment policies are also a key element of most efforts to produce flowers in developing countries. In many of the African countries, flower-growing is initiated when there is pressure to generate foreign exchange, often in order to pay debt. 'Non-traditional agricultural sectors' (to use the jargon of the international finance organisations) are then 'stimulated'. At the same time, under structural adjustment, the economy is entirely reshaped to create a larger role for the private sector and remove controls on their activities that may have existed. Most flower-production is undertaken by the private sector, and is aimed at foreign sales, so it is an ideal activity for encouragement in the course of structural adjustment.

Thus, funding that is aimed at providing the supporting infrastructure for the trade is often available from international sources. Roads need to be improved to get the produce to the airport; cooling and handling facilities must be in place there. In some cases, (see section on Zimbabwe) the growers themselves could benefit from foreign loans and grants and certainly many potential flower-growers have a need for feasibility studies. Some governments have set up bureaucracies to facilitate the trade, and these consume money. The Kenyans are reportedly building a storage facility at Nairobi airport. International support for such projects, we have been reliably informed, comes, not in the form of soft, but of hard loans, i.e. ones which involve high commercial interest rates.

The profits of the industry remains in the hands of private entrepreneurs, but, according to the ideology of structural adjustment, benefits will trickle down to the rest of the population via increased employment. There are some obvious areas of uncertainty in this economic blue-print: with so much of the profits diverted towards the purchase of foreign components for flower-growing, how much actually is taxable and thus available for the repayment of government-incurred debt? We have seen no analysis directed at answering this question, but it is possible that the current policy of structural adjustment may create a future problem of debt repayment. Or, if it does not, it doesn't seem to present a solution to the problem of existing debt. Moreover, in order to attract foreign private investment in the sector, many Third World countries are establishing tax holiday schemes for horticulture firms. Uganda, Tanzania and Zambia all offer 5 or 6 year tax-exemption conditions. Clearly, then, the only benefit that comes to the country from this industry is employment at the lowest rates of payment. Kenya is also reportedly going in the same direction.

Sources of funding

In the case of Zimbabwe, it is clear that governments of the 'developed' world and international banks are contributing heavily to a generalised programme of economic reform of which flower-growing is just one element. But that is a special case, as is described in the chapter on that country.

For other countries in Africa, the situation is less clear. Dutch businessmen in the flower-trade repeatedly refer to aid funds available from the World Bank, but the World Bank denies giving money to the sector. The same discrepancy occurs in the case of the European Union. Flower projects can indeed be financed under the Lomé Convention arrangements, but contrary to wide-spread assumption, this has not been done so far, according to EU official Bernard Caisso.

The World Bank's sister organisation, the International Finance Corporation, does list some small flower-growing projects in several countries among its portfolio. In 1991, it approved a million-dollar loan to a chrysanthemum farm in The Gambia, while in Kenya it lent a smaller amount to a rose and delphinium project. In 1993, it provided another half million to a Kenyan rose-grower, a lower amount to another in Uganda and a million to an anthurium farm in Fiji.

The US government has also channelled an unknown quantity of funds towards the flower sector in Latin America, the Caribbean and Africa. Much of this is in the generalised context of promoting export-agriculture, and in particular non-traditional crops; some specify flower-growing in particular. Our efforts to get comprehensive figures * for support of this sector from both USAID and the International Finance Corporation were not rewarded. Hence we can only extract conclusions from examples of assistance projects that we were able to get from other sources.

Development banks

Money reaches entrepreneurs in this area via regional development banks, which are supported by European development banks and other international financing organisations. One such is the Dutch Development Bank, the FMO, which may be an example of how the others work. The FMO is owned partly (51 per cent) by the Dutch government, partly by the large private banks of Holland. Traditionally it has been underwritten by the Dutch government, but, despite continuing public support, it is now run on strictly commercial lines. Hence, it is unclear whether financial support from such an institution can be described as development aid.

In the last decades, Martin de Jong of the FMO informed us, the Bank did 'entertain requests' from East African countries for loans to set up flower farms. It no longer does so, except in Zimbabwe. This official himself seemed to believe that it was not a secure enough sector for investment. But the FMO does give grants for feasibility studies in this sector and provides lines of credit connected to other finance organisations to which it is linked. In 1993, for instance, it provided a loan of nine million Dutch guilders to the Investment and Development Bank of Malawi for companies in agriculture and industry. The FMO itself is a shareholder in the Malawian Development Bank, along with other international finance organisations such as the Washington-based International Finance Corporation, a sister-organisation of the World Bank.

Technical assistance and expertise

It would appear that much of the aid in this sector takes the form of technical assistance: the financing of feasibility studies, training, advice. Below, we reproduce a part of the publicity material of one such programme

---

Kenya Export Development Support, a project funded by USAID

KEDS is a four-year project, implemented by a Development Alternatives Inc. consortium including Deloitte and Touche Ltd. The goals of KEDS are to increase employment and foreign exchange earnings in Kenya through increased non-traditional exports. The KEDS contract delivers short and long term technical assistance, commodities, training and analytical research to both the public and private sectors. We are working to reform the export policy environment, and also to increase the capability of businesses to respond to export opportunities. In June 1992, KEDS fielded a three-person long-term team.

The public sector

The KEDS Project has contributed to the improved export policy environment of 1993 in the following ways:

– KEDS has sponsored EPPO seminars in Nairobi, Kisumu and Mombasa to review Government of Kenya tax-based incentives and explore ways to improve infrastructural support in Kenya's communications, roads, rail sea and air transport;

– KEDS is performing a six-country Kenyan Export Competitiveness Study which will culminate in recommendations and national seminars on: legal and regulatory issues; institutional constraints; and factors of export production;

– A national workshop was held in February 1994 on Export Banking and Insurance to draft suggested amendments to the Banking Act and Insurance Act which will improve financial services to exporters.

The private sector

The Private Sector Component continued its program for client organisations: the (parastatal) Horticultural Crops Development Authority, the Fresh Produce Exporters Association of Kenya (FPEAK) and the Kenyan Association of Manufacturers (KAM), while launching the KEDS firm-level program. Recent achievements include:

– Desktop publishing software and training for FPEAK, HCDA and KAM staff to publish in-house newsletters; resource library management systems;

–FPEAK: Support to recruit and hire a Chief Executive; continued development of a Code of Practice; a workshop on International Trade Show Participation; an on-line market information system which faxes weekly market reports to members;

– HCDA: KEDS is working with a Task Force to finalise an extensive Export Crop Manual for producers and exporters; work is underway to develop a computer-based system to monitor horticultural export statistics;

– KAM: Support for KAM at Uganda's International Trade Fair led to a Kenyan Pavilion for 18 exporting firms and sales of over one million us dollars; two Export Finance for Manufacturers workshops were held in February 1994.

The European Union also has similar programmes of technical assistance. One example of this is provided by the work of an organisation called COLEACP, which, according to its publicity material, is a non-profit body set up under the aegis of the EU commission in 1973. This literature is extremely glossy and persuasive, and so are the experts supplied in the course of the technical assistance programmes. We attended a seminar organised by this body in the Caribbean, however, and we can categorically state that the information disseminated was extremely one-sided. The rise in supply of cut-flowers from the Third World was documented by impressive figures, and growers were exhorted to step up their production. Nothing was said about the reductions in price or the possibility of over-supply. We were left feeling that the small growers on these islands were being done a disservice. They could hardly imagine the scale of the efforts in larger Third World countries who were their competitors.

Some of the experts supplied by the 'missions' sent out to the Third World by the EU are former growers who subsequently sold their businesses at great profit to large multinational concerns. Their advice does not come cheap, but the would-be growers, who are often members of Third World elites, seem able to pay. One consultant told us his fees were 1,500 US dollars per day for a minimum of seven days and a first-class airline ticket to the country involved, as well as the costs involved in staying there. Often, the information offered by these consultants is dated and does not take account of local realities. We heard COLEACP's suave expert repeatedly stressing that Caribbean growers should stop trying to deliver their product to Northern European markets and try to enter through Southern Europe. However, there were no direct flights to Southern Europe from the Caribbean when he was saying this.

Another consultant we met enthusiastically talked about the potential earnings for small outgrowers in Africa and Latin America. But all of the hard-headed businessmen we interviewed insisted that the time had long passed when small growers could really make a profit in this business. This particular consultant had only become an expert in floriculture two years before. Before that, he had been an expert in vegetable horticulture. But, as he himself noted, that trade had turned out to be less profitable than expected. He insisted that prices in the flower industry were stable and even going up a bit, while the traders and the figures showed the opposite. When pressed on the subject of future profitability, he was quite airy, not to say irresponsible.

'I'm not God. You can never say what happens in the future', he remarked.

He was an employee of the Royal Tropical Institute of the Netherlands, which is 40-50 per cent financed by the Dutch government. His section of the Institute makes money for this body through the sort of consultancy services he provides for small growers in the Third World.

Concluding remarks

From our investigations, it would seem that much of the assistance given in this sector is by way of exhortations, encouragement and advice. The tangible money flows come largely through private investment by international capital, especially in Africa, facilitated by structural adjustment programmes. This means that the financial benefits of such investment are not likely to remain in the developing country, but absorbed into the international system. However governments in the Third World are being encouraged to invest in this sector through infrastructural development and to forgo tax revenues in the hope of long-term benefits. Our prognosis about the long-term profitability of the trade due to falling prices, rising supply and its vulnerability on a number of fronts makes this seem a very dubious development strategy.

PART II

National Flower Sectors

CHAPTER 6

The Case of Colombia
Labour Conditions, Health and Environment

A success story, they call it. And to be sure, not every country is up to what Colombia has achieved: seizing 10 per cent of an international market and becoming second only to the long-time market leader. In flowers, Colombia has definitely hit the big time.

But make a tour around the place where it all happens, the plains (or savannah) of Bogotá. Listen to the people involved in flower production. Visit a local doctor. Open a tap. Interview one or two mayors. And you start to wonder: is *this* what a success story looks like?

Some figures first. In the plains of Bogotá, where four out of five Colombian flowers are grown, between 3,500 and 4,000 hectares are dedicated to this crop. In 1991, just over 100,000 tons were exported, with a value of 267 million dollars. Out of every four cut flowers sold to United States consumers, one was grown in this area. These figures make cut flowers Colombia's fifth (legal*) export product and the third export crop after coffee and bananas.

---

* The illegal trade in cocaine is linked up with the flowers exports in several ways. Several times, drugs hidden in loads of flowers were captured at US airports. More importantly, narcodollars are syphoned into the sector to be laundered. 'You can tell', one Dutch source says. 'When you see a small farm with a palace-like house and the guy is vague about his other business ventures, you just *know*.' A colleague-specialist explains how it works: 'They state fictitious export volumes, higher than the real figures. The non-existent payment for the non-existent goods which does however appear in the books is the amount laundered.' If correct, this means that the actual export figures may be lower than the ones presented here. By how much? Nobody knows.

Employment estimates vary. The Colombian Flower Exporters' Association (Asocolflores) puts it at 70,000 directly employed by the growers and another 60,000 depending indirectly on the sector, such as truck drivers and plastic factory labourers. Children and other relatives of the workers are not included. Other estimates are higher.

The business is doing well. 'Up to a few years ago, the flower growers were used to extremely high profit rates', says Jairo Ernesto Luna, a doctor involved in a multidisciplinary Bogotá National University investigation of the sector. 'Since growing flowers fitted into the government's policy of stimulating non-traditional exports, they got cheap credits and exemption from tariffs for the inputs they imported. Recent economic reforms have reduced their profitability by doing away with some subsidies.'

Wages and labour conditions

However, and in spite of these economic accomplishments, 'even in the context of Colombia's nationwide poverty, and taking into account the fact that it is still a developing country, the poverty of the savannah is extreme'.[22]

A major reason for this are low wage levels. Contrary to employers' claims, unskilled labourers tend to earn hardly more than the official minimum wage, about 120 US dollars a month, plus social security payments and one extra month's salary a year. There should be bonuses for overtime on top of that[23], but these are not always paid.[24]

It is widely admitted that the cost of maintaining a family in Colombia is three times the minimum wage. Food used to be inexpensive in the region, which was the granary (and potato-barn) for the city of Bogotá. Nowadays, according to a British source, foodstuffs cost about half the UK equivalent, and more than that for protein-rich products such as chicken. In other agro-industrial sectors, such as banana and oil palm plantations, trade unions have succeeded in getting wages up to, or near, that necessary level.[25] Flower companies have so far resisted demands to follow suit.

Women, who make up about 60 per cent of the work force on flower farms, are mostly in the low-paying unskilled jobs, whereas many of the male workers hold positions as fumigators and supervisors or have white collar posts, with the better wages that come with these. It would be incorrect to assume that only these men, unlike their female colleagues, have families to support – many of the women are the sole income-earners in their households.

Also, it is questionable to categorize the female labourers' jobs as unskilled. Recognizing a crop pest at an early stage, one of their tasks, requires a lot of experience, as does, to a lesser extent, the sorting, classifying and packaging of the harvest. On the other hand, spraying pesticides onto the beds, even though it certainly *should* be skilled work, is often carried out by men who have not received the 120 hours' training prescribed by Colombian law.

Low wages are not the result of short hours. Whereas in other agricultural sectors labour time is under the legal standard of 48 hours a week, in the flower industry it tends to exceed that, especially in peak seasons: before Christmas, before Valentine's Day, before Mother's Day. In those periods, people work seven days a week, up to twelve, sometimes even fifteen hours a day. Allegedly, overtime work is optional, but refusing to do so is virtually equivalent to resigning.[26] Long hours are particularly burdensome for the sizeable group of single mothers engaged in this work, who are continually faced with the problem of finding someone to take care of their children.

Work pressure is high and rising. In 1980, each worker was in charge of ten beds of flowers a day. Twelve years on, this number had increased to sixteen, eighteen, twenty-four, in some places even thirty. This is probably one of the reasons why the age of workers preferred by employers has been going down, from people in their thirties to those under thirty.[27]

There is also a small, but significant, number of minors working in the industry. In a recent survey, 9 out of 55 companies employed at least one. One estimate puts their total number at 300. Sometimes even children as young as seven years old are brought into the greenhouses by women who fear they might otherwise fail to fulfil their quotas. This would lead to wage deductions.[28]

Job stability, which used to be precarious in that employers would seize upon any pretext to rid themselves of certain workers, is now non-existent for ever more people in the sector. In 1990, in accordance with IMF advice, parliament passed an act to 'flexibilise the labour market'. Law 50, as it is known, allows temporary contracts for three to six months, during which period no social security contributions have to be paid. At the end of the term, the employee can be laid off with no reasons given at all – not even bogus reasons, as used to be common practice. This has virtually stripped workers of what little rights they had.

Flower growers compare negatively with other sectors. 'They are a different sort of entrepreneurs', Jairo Ernesto Luna explains. 'The coffee farmers are people from that soil, from the region, with a sense of responsibility towards their surroundings. The flower growers, on the other hand, arrive in the region to invest in something profitable.'

Health and pesticides

Headaches, nausea, skin irritation and rash, dizziness, miscarriages, premature and still births, malformations in babies, poisoning of sucklings, hyperactivity of the bronchial system, asthma, neurological problems, allergies, impaired eyesight and several sorts of cancers: talk to doctors and workers in the Bogotá plains, and you hear long lists of ailments and afflictions. No, they cannot say for sure that the high incidence of these is due to the presence of and work at the flower plantations. As a matter of fact, since nobody has ever bothered to conduct a comprehensive health survey in the area, they cannot even claim that there is a scientifically proven, statistically significant higher incidence. *But they can tell.* They know a health crisis when they see one – or rather, live one. And they will not accept supervisors downplaying their complaints by saying, as they tend to, 'You're dizzy? S'pose you didn't have a proper breakfast.'[29] Although, of course, widespread malnutrition does make the flower workers more vulnerable to any health hazard.

In 1983, a small sample of forty women workers was asked if they had health problems. Just five of them did not. Their list of complaints reads as follows: headaches (26 cases), skin problems (22), conjunctivitis (18), kidney ailments (17), vomiting (12), dizziness (10), menstruation problems (9), numb limbs (7), back pain (7), impaired eyesight (6), general weakness (6), diarrhoea (6), stomach acidity (4), anxiety (4), vaginal secretion (4), breathlessness (4), stomach pains (4), fainting (3), miscarriage (3), insomnia (3), tight chest (2), neck pains (1), premature birth (1). Certainly not all complaints are directly work-related; the

Bogotá plain, with its poverty, dust and overall contamination is an unhealthy place anyway. But 179 complaints in just forty persons is an alarming number.

The most dangerous thing about flower growing is the extensive use of pesticides to wipe out diseases (in the plants), fungi and bugs and to disinfect the soil before planting it. According to the government agency regulating pesticide admission into the country, the ICA, 18.75 kilos per hectare were used in floriculture in 1990. This is equivalent to 10.04 kilos of active ingredients. However, independent researchers cite far higher figures. According to one of them, about 70 kilos are applied to every hectare; this data probably refers to gross amount, as opposed to active ingredient. The source concedes that this is not excessive in international terms.[30] But another researcher calculates that the average use of pesticides is 333,6 kilos per hectare, containing about 180 kilos of active ingredients.[31]

In Colombia and elsewhere, floriculture is the one agricultural sector that consumes most pesticides. This is not just because the crop is vulnerable. More importantly, the United States and Japan maintain extremely strict phytosanitary (plant health) requirements, which are regarded by the outside world as a non-tariff import barrier: one little bug can cause an entire load to be refused entry to the country. To live up to these requirements, producers wield the spray-can liberally. Since the product is not eaten, chemical residues are not considered to be a problem. The Dutch flower auctions in Holland, with their pivotal position in world trade, maintain the American and Japanese requirements, to make sure every load of flowers they handle can potentially go to any destination. Therefore, the Japanese and American standards in practice dictate the pesticide regimes throughout the world, from Holland to Kenya and Colombia.

Even more worrying than the sheer amounts are the types of chemicals applied. Notoriously dangerous substances such as aldrin and dieldrin, banned in many countries, were legal in Colombia up to early 1994, when the Ministry of Health forbade the use of these two and five other so-called organochlorides. A step to be applauded, for sure, just like the prohibition, years earlier, of the carcinogenic fungicide captafol. Unfortunately, there are recent reports of this pesticide still being used.[32] And organophosphates, another family of chemicals that is even more toxic than organochlorides, have not been outlawed yet.

Worldwide, there is less than comprehensive knowledge about the health effects of pesticides in general, and of pesticides used on flowers in greenhouses in particular. Since the effects of these chemicals tend to be long-term rather than immediate, it has proven difficult to conclusively identify links between cause and effect. The knowledge available is generally not reassuring. Especially those in WHO categories IA and IB (extremely and highly dangerous) have very serious effects when they enter the body through skin, mucous membranes or stomach. Among the most serious dangers are leukaemia and other types of cancer, infertility and damage to foetuses. Since floriculture is a comparatively small sector, chemicals used here are often not tailor-made for it. In the isolated environment of greenhouses, exposure of workers to the chemicals can be expected to be more intense.[33] Both factors pose additional risks.

In Colombia, as in many other Latin American countries, pesticides are often not handled with the care advised. As mentioned earlier on, fumigators tend not to receive the training required by both national law and WHO standards. Not wearing the protective clothing that the pesticide manufacturers recommend seems to be the rule rather than the exception. And in stark disregard of prescriptions, which insist on a waiting period of 12 to 48 hours, depending on the exact substance, workers are sent back into the greenhouses within hours of spraying. Within minutes even, as the following testimony illustrates:

'As soon as the pesticide applicator comes out, the women go in again. The flower beds are still sticky and moist with the pesticides and we have no gloves and no suitable working clothes to protect at least our clothing. We get greasy all over with pesticides.'[34]

'Many growers are hardly aware of the dangers that pesticides pose', says doctor Luna. 'It's not necessarily ill will on their side. They didn't mind us seeing workers getting back into the greenhouses within an hour after spraying. They thought it natural.'

Two more examples show the extremes of carelessness with which hazardous chemicals were and are handled in some places. A woman with fifteen years' experience in floriculture:

'It was always said, the one [pesticide] which smelled stronger was the most dangerous, so the owners would say: "This doesn't smell so it's safe".'[35]

And in the early days of flower growing in Colombia, before lunch, women would clean their hands with the same sponges used to clean the carnation petals, arguing that even though the pesticides used for the leaves might be aggressive, those for the blooms couldn't possibly be.[36]

Faced with criticisms about hazardous pesticide use, Asocolflores's president, Felipe Zuleta Lleras, retorted that European manufacturers were to blame, not Colombian flower growers. (He even went as far as claiming that the criticisms had forced his organization to launch a countercampaign, the high costs of which made it difficult to finance social development plans.)[37]

Working conditions also put people's health at risk. Standing, bending over, squatting or kneeling for hours on end does not do anybody's back and legs any good – and it is certainly not the sort of position that makes a pregnant woman feel comfortable. (Pregnant women often try to conceal their state for fear of dismissal, in spite of protective legislation.) Temperatures equally take their toll. Greenhouses are naturally hot, sometimes very hot. Sorting rooms, on the other hand, have to be cool, especially for roses, which feel best at 12°C – unlike the women handling them. The cold storage facilities, finally, tend to be chilly, hardly above freezing-point. All three temperatures are unpleasant, but worst off are the workers involved in taking the flowers from the greenhouses to the sorting rooms or from these to the cold stores.

Nearly all flower companies have resident doctors, who conduct regular blood tests to trace toxic substances. However, the results are rarely given to the workers. Some companies have occupational health committees. In a recent survey by the National University of Bogotá, 40 out of 55 companies based in the town of Madrid claimed they did. Further research revealed that 26 of these claims were false.

The health effects of the flower plantations reach beyond the workers themselves. The pesticides that stick to the workers' skin can easily be conveyed to their children. It has also been established that the breast-milk of the workers can be contaminated.[38]

And pesticides find their way into people's bodies in even more tortuous ways. Some companies sell flower stems as fodder, which is eaten by cows, which turn it into milk and meat, which is drunk and eaten by local people.[39]

Water

The inhabitants of the savannah have learnt by experience that flowers need water – just like they themselves. The enormous expansion of the crop has pushed water consumption beyond the level the region can sustain. The ground water level has sunk, rivers have dwindled. People and flowers compete for water, and flowers get the better of it.[40]

As a consequence of the general shortage, which in some years is aggravated by drought, getting clean water and conserving it in buckets has become a daily time-consuming nuisance for a great number people. In many villages, opening a tap yields the desired result for a few hours each week only. To the eye it does, at any rate. A chemical analysis would show most of the water to be unreliable. Many companies do not have water treatment plants, so that pesticide run-offs reach the rivers and ground water. The water company prefers to simply *assume* the absence of pesticide residues.

Public protest against water shortage has been widespread in the savannah. Up to 1992, there had been 28 local *paros* (standstill of public life through strikes and road-blocks) in just a few years. The water shortages and the sinking ground water table have already prompted some municipalities, such as Tenjo, to limit further expansion of flower growing. The mayor and the town council feel access of the public to drinking water should have priority. In other places, such as Funza, where the mayor is a flower grower himself, such a step is not to be expected.

Trade unions

Why don't trade unions do something about all this? After all, Colombia has a long tradition of labour organization and conflict. Collective bargaining is a common practice in the country. The right to organize is upheld by Colombian law.

As a matter of fact, 20 per cent of workers in the flower sector is unionized. Not a very high figure, maybe, but the real problem lies elsewhere. Employers will only tolerate unions that are affiliated to the Ultracun federation[41] – the yellow ones, as researcher Luna calls them.

Workers are discouraged from trying to set up independent unions, to put it mildly. Among the friendlier dissuasive methods are offering them better jobs or premiums or talking them into joining the existing employer-friendly unions. More common than the carrot is the stick: dismissal. First the 'rabble-rousers' are fired; later on, if deemed necessary, the other workers involved go the same way. Sometimes, fake reasons are given, such as 'undisciplined conduct', 'laziness' or 'restructuring of the company'. In other cases, the management simply cites the attempt to establish an independent trade union as the justification. At a more general level of discourse the companies refer to the workers' alleged communist leanings and the risk of guerrilla infiltration.

The case of Monteverde, a company in Funza, where over twenty workers were fired in September 1993, is a textbook example. Management clamped down on workers who tried to spread the word of a trade union being established and on some others who were somehow associated with the initiative. To a few employees the true reason was given, other were accused of having given a bad example or of having torn out plants. Several of them had been with the company for over six years.[42] They lodged a complaint with the Court for labour disputes, which ruled that the dismissal had not been collective and was therefore legal.

Once workers have been fired, they are likely to get on the computerized black list that is said to circulate among companies. Even their relatives may face problems in finding jobs. The high number of women working in the sector, and single mothers in particular, is considered another barrier to a high degree of unionization. As a matter of fact, according to Luna, one of the reasons for employers hiring women in the early years of Colombian floriculture (80 per cent used to be female) was that their humble peasant origins and limited education made them less likely to unionize. Nowadays, that has changed somewhat. This, added to the compulsory 84 days' maternity leave that has been introduced into Colombia's labour code, has led employers' preference to shift to men.

As to the unions' difficulty in getting women to participate, they also have themselves to blame. They do not give any attention to how they could make it easier for these women to do so, for instance by convening meetings at suitable hours.

Finally, the increasing practice of temporary contracts is an obstacle for workers defending their interests in an organized manner.

'Asocolflores claims companies respect the right of unionization', Luna says. 'But this right does not apply to temporary-contract worker. So if they have ever less permanent people, what meaning does this right have?'

Firing people for fake offenses, for founding a trade union, for pregnancy: all of this is forbidden in Colombia. But employers can be sure of impunity for these and other infractions of the labour code as well as health regulation. The Ministries of Labour and Health are underfunded, understaffed (in the entire savannah, there are only two labour inspectors) and in quite a few instances uninterested. The latter can be explained by the government's unmitigated support for the flower sector, which is among the few Colombian industries seen as capable of facing the sharpening international competition.

An exception to this blind backing was the admission by minister of Labour Posada de la Peña, in 1992, that the flower entrepreneurs had preserved some of the 'feudal attitude of the ancient *hacienda* owners'.

Criticisms and campaigns

These health problems, environmental damage and bad labour relations have drawn sharp criticism, both domestically and from European NGOs and the European Parliament. Since the late eighties, several organizations in Germany have been campaigning in cooperation with Colombian trade unions (in particular the Interinstitutional Flowers Commission) for better conditions in the flower industry. In 1994, the British charity Christian Aid also took up the cause. Its involvement is more directly relevant, in that Britain is twice as big a market for Colombian flowers as Germany. However, the entire European Union buys only half the amount of Colombian flowers the United States and Canada import (in value terms).[43] In these countries, there is no public interest in the issue.

Unlike with other product-related campaigns, no consumer boycott is being advocated. Rather, the European NGOs and the Colombian trade unions demand from the employers that they observe Colombian law regarding labour conditions, pesticide use and environmental care. So far, their pleas have largely fallen on deaf ears. A recent proof of this was the performance of Asocolflores at the European Parliament's hearings, in April 1994, about the Colombian flower sector. The Asocolflores representatives simply denied most of the claims, alleging that both the Colombian state and the companies themselves are doing their very best to steadily improve labour and other conditions. To substantiate these rebuttals, they had brought two leaders of 'yellow' trade unions.

The hearing was a follow-up to a 1993 European Parliament resolution mentioning Colombian flower growing, along with Chinese forced labour and Indian child labour, as examples of human rights violations in export-oriented production. The boycott threat that seemed to be looming never materialized, but the NGO campaign and the European Parliament interest put together does seem to have prompted the German flower import and wholesale association, BGI, and Asocolflores to draft a Clean Flowers Declaration, which was signed in September 1994. Colombian companies subscribing to the declaration proclaim that they will observe their country's labour, pesticide and environmental laws, thereby adding their name to a white list. They also accept independent inspections. The German companies, on their side, undertake to import flowers from companies on the white list only.

The Declaration does not imply that Asocolflores has recognized the charges against the sector. Rather, they still claim that the problems are blown up, also suggesting that most critics are communist agitators, bent on damaging Colombia's economic success and reputation abroad. To refute the criticisms against them, they usually emphasize the responsible management on certain farms, including proper treatment of labourers, good working conditions and careful pesticide handling.

These farms do exist, among both small, medium and large companies. One source goes to considerable lengths to praise Rosex SA for being 'a model employer – evidence that not all Colombian growers find it necessary to exploit their workers'. Every worker has an indefinite contract and is affiliated to social security; fumigators get adequate training, proper protective clothing, are rotated to reduce exposure to pesticides and get monthly medical check-ups; and the typical petty restrictions (certain hours for going to the toilet, prohibitions on occasionally talking to colleagues etc.) are missing. Manager Guillermo León claims that his company is not exceptional at all, but 'across the savannah, this statement is greeted with some scepticism'.[44]

Also, Asocolflores has been instrumental in a couple of positive developments. In their research lab in Bogotá, the organization helps develop new methods for crop protection and keeps track of the latest international developments in pest management. In another field, Asocolflores members are providing aid to 250 state nurseries, as well as contributing to local housing programmes and building a health centre. A park is being built and a special social fund has been established.[45]

Both Rosex's and Asocolflores's efforts are important: they show that the sector is perfectly capable, financially and otherwise, of mending its ways – if only it is determined to do so.

CHAPTER 7

The Case of Kenya
Where Have All the Profits Gone?

'In Kenya, horticulture has become very important. Kenya is an agricultural country and we depend on agricultural exports to earn foreign exchange.'
L. W. Waithaka, Technical Services Manager, Horticultural Development Crops Authority, 1992

The home of the largest carnation farm on the globe, Kenya, has over 800 hectares of land planted with blooms for export. 600 million Kenyan flowers (25,000 tons) went to the international market in 1993. One farm alone dispatches 5 plane-loads of flowers per week in the high season while a transport firm ships another 12 plane-loads, making this East African country, as one Dutch banker put it, 'the most interesting producing country in the developing world.'

But the profits of all this do not remain in Kenya.

Production of cut flowers and cutfoliage in Kenya in hectares

Type of flower	1987	1988	1989	1990	1991
Spray carnations	120	145	157	182	220
Standard carnations	36	50	19	53	27
Roses	16	25	21	27	47
Alstroemeria	48	55	68	82	50
Statice	128	197	209	101	119
Others	283	192	203	94	175
Total	631	664	677	539	638

Source Horticultural Crops Development Authority and Ministry of Agriculture, Livestock Development and Marketing Production Statistics, Kenya.

Major export commodities 1989-1993 by volume

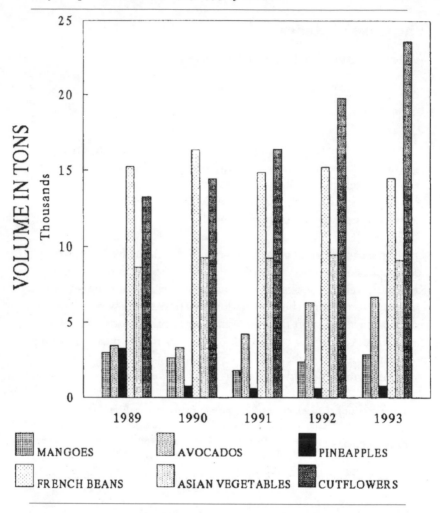

VOLUME IN TONS
Thousands

MANGOES

AVOCADOS

PINEAPPLES

FRENCH BEANS

ASIAN VEGETABLES

CUTFLOWERS

Source Horticultural Crops Development Authority Statistics, 1989-1993.

Foreign ownership

'Most of the farms belong to outsiders, not nationals', stated a veteran in the flower business there.

Several reports confirmed this. Fifty per cent of the 45 flower companies in Kenya are owned by foreigners. These are the ones which produce the impressive export figures. Sulmac, for example, which exports well over 250 million stems (8,000 tons) each year, is owned by Unilever, the giant Anglo-Dutch multinational. It had a turnover of over 20 million pounds sterling in 1991. Del Monte, the US food multinational, also owns a flower company in Kenya. The rest of the big farms are dominated by Dutch, German and Swiss investors.

'Of the list of registered growers, seven are above ten hectares', the head of Sulmac told a seminar in Zimbabwe in 1992, 'and of these seven, three have their own handling facilities (cold store, etc) at Jomo Kenyatta International Airport'.

Thirty-five per cent of the other farms are owned by white Kenyans. Only three per cent belong to black Kenyans.

'These are the kind of people who already have some money and are looking for a product they can export', stated a Dutch banker who handles the foreign accounts of several Kenyan farm-owners. 'After all, it takes one million guilders (about 600,000 US dollars) to develop one hectare of flowers.'

Statements from an interview with a senior manager of one multinational firm (name withheld for obvious reasons)

'All the big companies have been harping how good this trade was for Kenya in getting foreign exchange. But the only reason people encouraged Kenya and other developing countries to get involved was the high costs of producing in Europe. The developed countries are trying to shift production because of the price of land and labour there. The flower business brought some employment into Kenya, but that was all. Most of the money made does not stay here.

'They remit most of their profits out of the country. And then there is the high cost of the imputs in this business. The biggest single cost is air freight. That is 50 per cent of the wholesale price. We don't have any local airline carrying the flowers. Then we have to pay 10 per cent commission to the middlemen in Europe. The Dutch are the biggest middlemen. Their auctions are very expensive. We have to pay 6 per cent commission and 1.5 per cent for advertising, handling, preparing the flowers for auction and things like the hiring of buckets. And Kenyan flowers are priced lower than Dutch flowers, because they are regarded as less fresh. But Kenyan growers have lost a lot of money when they don't go through the auctions.

'And there are the costs of plants, which come from Europe. Even if we propagate them locally, we have to pay royalties. If you buy a rose plant for 1.20 US dollar, half of that price is royalties. And you still have to pay the price of flying it to Kenya. That plant will last for 6-8 years and you will get 6-10 flowers per year from it. And we often get swindled by suppliers of plant materials, who sell us plants which don't grow or produce properly.

'Then there are chemicals, fertilisers and fuels, all of which have to be imported. And the costs of consultants, growers and expatriate managers. These demand very high salaries; they are not cheap.

'The only local imput is labour. What it all boils down to is exploitation of these poor countries.

'If you, the producer, earn 15 per cent, you are lucky. You are doing very well. You have a lot of risks involved. There are a lot of problems with airfreight. Then there is the weather risk. And the market itself is a high-risk one. There's a saying in the flower trade in Holland that when women are naked on the beach, the trade is in the gutter. Once the weather is good, housewives forget about interior decor and go to the beach, so there's no market.

'In general, this trade is going down. Kenya saw this tremendous increase in production 7 to 8 years ago. But in the last three or four years, it hasn't done as well as before. The market is saturated. Other African countries – Uganda, Tanzania – are giving 6-year tax holidays to companies investing in floriculture. They are getting money from organisations for development aid like USAID (US) and GTZ (Germany).

'And what happens when big countries like India and China get into the market?'

Export of cut flowers and cut foliage from Kenya 1980-91

Year	Total Fresh Hort. Exports Tons	Cut Flower Exports Tons	% Quantity Cut Flowers	Total FOB* Value Fresh Hort Produce K£ '000	FOB* Value Cut Flowers K£ '000	%Value Cut Flowers
1980	22,266	3,788	17.0	11,353	4,924	43.4
1981	23,532	3,981	17.4	12,581	5,175	41.1
1982	24,597	4,319	17.5	13,634	5,615	41.2
1983	28,850	5,209	18.1	17,529	7,293	41.6
1984	31,298	6,961	22.9	20,793	8,701	41.8
1985	30,002	7,474	24.9	23,462	10,464	44.6
1986	36,211	8,265	22.8	31,518	12,397	39.3
1987	36,557	8,613	23.6	53,711	25,119	46.8
1988	59,119	10,946	18.5	66,397	31,744	47.8
1989	49,504	13,245	26.8	72,002	36,424	50.6
1990	49,147	14,423	29.3	83,924	43,268	51.6
1991	49,848	16,405	32.9	98,101	49,215	50.2

* FOB = Free on Board

Source Export Statistics, Horticultural Crops Development Authority Kenya.

Dubious business practice

Allegations of dubious – and even illegal – business practice riddle Kenyan flower-lore. The whole thing began with a Danish billionaire who left his own country, it is said, because of some problem with the authorities there but still managed to get Danish development aid money to develop a chrysanthemum company called DCK East Africa. One of his partners was a white government minister – reputedly the minister of agriculture – who died suddenly when a charter plane carrying DCK's flowers crashed on the way to Israel. Apparently there was a bomb on board; rumour has it that the bombing was linked to arms trading.

From these beginnings, the floriculture trade never looked back. Till today, many businessmen involved with Kenyan flowers have the air of cowboys in the wild west: engaging adventurers who thrive on risk and defy conventions. Exactly the type to ignore, flout or find ways around any legal or safety regulations that might get in the way.

Some Kenyan insiders are skeptical of the value of their involvement with the African country.

'The trade has not made any substantial contribution via taxes', stated a senior official of one flower-firm in 1994. 'There has been some indirect taxation on imputs brought into the country, but that is all.'

As early as 1977, the Nairobi Times published a report accusing horticultural exporters of defrauding the Kenyan Central Bank by failing to declare their full profits and thus depriving the country of tax revenue. It cited an official of the Horticultural Development Crops Authority which was trying to bring the trade under its jurisdiction.

'Among the firms in the game', the newspaper stated, 'are big horticultural concerns owning large farms in Kenya and who have other business interests overseas... Echaria further revealed that some exporters were engaged in some form of conspiracy with some importers through which the country is losing substantial foreign exchange. Some exporters declare less value for their exports on the understanding that their trading partners overseas would bank extra revenue realised overseas or invest it in joint ventures there.

'Other tricks some horticultural firms have employed to make extra earnings that are never brought back to Kenya involve deliberate suppression of producer prices and, through so doing, undervaluing their exports while they sell produce in overseas markets exorbitantly.'

According to this report, the horticultural traders (including vegetable and fruit exporters) had cheated the country of 500 million shillings since they began business in Kenya. DCK East Africa owed 150 million shillings to the central bank, it stated.

A year later, that company's name had changed to Sulmac. It had been sold to Brooke Bond, the British tea and coffee company which had had plantations in Kenya since colonial times.

'Brooke Bond was ripped off in that deal', says an insider.

However, the firm had made a great deal of money in Kenya. According to one foreigner, it wanted to put some of this back into the country. Nationals charge, however, that it only got involved in the flower game in order to repatriate profits from its tea business out of the country, for after independence, the government had passed laws against the remittance of money abroad. In 1984, Brooke Bond was bought by the giant food company, Unilever.

Importers of cut flowers from Kenya, 1991

Country	Quantity (tons)	% of Kenyan flower export
Netherlands	9,463	57.7
Germany	4,683	28.5
United Kingdom	1,223	7.5
Switzerland	414	2.5
France	156	1.0

Source Export Statistics, Horticultural Crops Development Authority, Kenya.

As the trade bloomed, the Horticultural Crops Development Authority kept trying to stem the leakage of foreign exchange. But monitoring the flower trade is a virtually impossible task for any government, particularly one in the Third World. It is, of necessity, highly integrated with international business. Banking must be done outside of the country because of the gigantic proportion of the proceeds which have to be paid for imputs: capital equipment, chemicals, the services of consutants and experts, planting materials, royalties, freight charges. Just one branch of the Rabobank in Holland has 15 Kenyan flower growers using its payment system.

There is therefore infinite room for falsifying of declarations to the authorities in the country of production. Often, the value of the product is only determined when it appears before the clock at the electronic auction in Holland, and is dependent on the condition of the flowers on arrival and the volume of supply on that day. Or a large per cent of the wholesale price goes to importers and wholesalers in Europe. The sector is simply too modern for governments to monitor, too much a part of the current culture of international business, which defies the control of any state, however large and powerful.

'In the early eighties', the manager of a large firm told Gerda van Roozendaal, 'the Kenyan state tried to get the flower sector into the straitjacket of a marketing board. Companies have prevented this'.

Having failed to beat the system of international business, the government decided to join it. According to Waithaka, it instituted a research programme and advisory service for small scale growers and began constructing a large cold storage facility at Nairobi airport in 1992. The road from one of the key production areas, Naivasha, has also been improved, and, according to a report from a local journalist, in 1991 the army bulldozed 40 acres of tropical forest to make way for a rose plantation.

'The industry is receiving much attention from both the private and public sectors and many more people are investing in the floriculture trade', Waithaka observed at a seminar in Zimbabwe in 1992.

These investors, trade insiders keep repeating, now include the country's president and central bank governor. Even the non-controversial trade journal, Vakblad voor de Bloemisterij, states that the 'people in power' now have large stakes in the business in this 'little volcano where political murders are part of the normal culture'.

'Companies appear and disappear all the time', observed an official of a large foreign firm. 'They are often set up by high government and bank officials, the latter lending money to themselves.'

Monthly Kenyan flower exports in 1991

Month	Quantity (tons)	% Total
January	2,364	14.4
February	2,251	13.7
March	1,906	11.6
April	878	5.4
May	740	4.5
June	133	0.8
July	137	0.8
August	343	2.1
September	1,168	7.1
October	1,937	11.8
November	1,839	11.2
December	2,708	16.5

Source Export Statistics, Horticultural Crops Development Authority, Kenya.

The workers

Such entrepreneurs hold the fate of over 30,000 employees in their hands. During interview after interview with Dutch businessmen involved in the Kenyan trade, the low cost of labour in Kenya was described in terms of delighted wonder. Thus, there have been a number of enthusiastic articles in the Dutch press about the glories of shifting production to Africa, where a worker can legally be paid less than 1.00 US dollar per day.

But employers also provide housing and medical benefits, they are quick to point out. Sulmac, for example, publishes colour brochures showing exotic pictures of native homes on its plantations, complete with medical clinic, primary school and sports facilities. There is no mention that they must provide these by Kenyan law. This is a legacy of the old colonial plantation system – if the company did not provide these things it would be forced to pay the workers a housing allowance. Moreover, the workers would have to travel long distances to work which would disturb the pace of production.

'It is all militarised like a parade ground, in the spray carnation area [where mainly women work]', stated David Gray. 'It has to be fairly regimented, surveyed and laid out in advance.'

The brochures also neglect to mention that one third of Sulmac's 4,500 workers are not entitled to these benefits, being occasional labour employed only when needed. Nor do they reflect the fact that employees end up with no place to live when they can no longer work. They may prefer to have the housing allowance instead, and gradually use this to acquire a permanent home, rather than live with their children in the one room the company provides and share washing facilities with 72 others. But they have no choice.

Sulmac's publicity material shows creches, schools, playgrounds, a choir and football team, without mentioning that half of Sulmac's labourers are women, who, as the company's head, David Gray, put it during a speech in 1992, 'do a lot of the hard work in Kenya'. Providing child care is vital to keeping them at work.

The company's organisation brings to mind the classic colonial plantation, which is exactly its origins in the tea sector. Its total domination of workers' lives is a dubious benefit. Sulmac is able to make crucial decisions on how employees' children are reared from an early age, what they are taught in school, what level of medical aid they are given, what kind of family planning advice...

For an employee to leave Sulmac would amount to her giving up all her life-support systems. To stay means being immersed in the total culture of Sulmac, working at piece-rates in this stressful, time-dominated environment. And many of the benefits now being provided may be under threat. The government's current policy of economic liberalisation involves scrapping labour guidelines which have forced companies to invest in provisions for employees.

At the same time, profit margins are dwindling and growth in this sector is slowing down, as Kenyan flower prices have lost 25 per cent in recent years with the increasing supply from other Third World countries.

Local producers

'Professional black men are now growing millions of roses', observed Cor van Duyn, a Dutch businessman who has long been involved in the Kenyan trade.

Cash-hungry Farmers Ditch Food for Flowers
by Pamphil Kweyuh

'Flower-buyers will follow you to the bedroom', says Mwangi Mucene of Kinangop in Kenya. 'On this one and a half acre plot, I can grow over 20,000 flowers and earn 10,000 shillings in one season.'

Previously, he used to grow potatoes, the staple food of people here. But he had to transport the bulky produce over bad roads to the market. With flowers, the buyers come to him. It's no surprise: when they buy a carnation from Mucene for fifty Kenyan cents, they re-sell it to exporters in Nairobi for five times that.

All over Kenya, farmers have switched from growing potatoes, carrots, maize and cabbages, which local people eat, to the production of flowers or luxury vegetables like French beans, which are flown to Europe. In the Vihiga district, for example, one of the most densely-populated regions of the country, no food for local consumption is now grown. In other traditional agricultural areas, food production has halved, as farmers climb on the export bandwagon.

Now they can pay school fees for most of their children, replace their thatched huts with corrugated-iron-roofed houses and have piped water in their homes. The only problem is that food prices are doubling every two years. Maize, which many of them once grew, now has to be trucked in from 200 kilometres away.

Horticulture has overtaken coffee and become the country's second export commodity after tea. In 1967 – when the Horticulture Crop Development Authority (HCDA) was set up to develop, promote and regulate this industry – most Kenyans didn't know what a French bean was. The country was then exporting around 1,480 tonnes of horticulture products. By 1992, Kenya was shipping out 57,000 tons of flowers and luxury vegetables, from which it earned 78 million US dollars. By the turn of the century, horticulture is expected to bring in 406 million US dollars per year.

The aim is to cover Kenya's 250 million dollar trade deficit, caused by plummeting prices for its traditional export crops – coffee and tea. Among horticultural products, flowers are the biggest earner. Some 35 per cent of this export trade is in flowers; they account for more than half of this sector's income. So the export trade is expanding more in this direction and tea plantations are being converted to flowers.

In 1991, the army bulldozed 100 acres of tropical forest to make way for Sian Roses. Large quantities of water from Lake Naivasha, the only fresh-water lake in Rift valley, are pumped to the precious export crop. Ecologists fear that the lake will dry up and warn that massive amounts of dangerous pesticides and fertilisers are draining into it from the rose plantations.

Multinational food companies – such as Britain's Brooke Bond and the US's Del Monte – pioneered the export-oriented production. It proved so lucrative that rich land-owners, the government and even small-scale farmers jumped on the bandwagon. Artificial irrigation was needed to make thousands of acres of arid and semi-arid lands productive. In one region – Perkerra – the shallow irrigation trenches have become breeding grounds for mosquitoes, and 60 to 100 people have been treated for malaria at the local clinic. Land clearance for 'new farmers', i.e. horticulturists, on the slopes of Mt Kenya has destroyed the catchment areas for rivers in the district. Traditional farmers below are without water for their food crops, which causes food prices in the area to double every two years.

The whole export business has now run into problems, however. Europe has been trying to regulate imports that have high pesticide residue levels since January this year. Kenyan producers are major culprits. According to the United Nations Environmental Programme, they use over 1,500 pesticides, most of which are unregistered.

A 1992 study revealed that farmers in Kenya make extensive use of several carcinogenic chemicals, including Carbosulfan 25ec, which has been denied registration in the US eight times. Banned in Malaysia and Panama, this pesticide is sprayed on vegetables, french beans, citrus fruits, mangoes and flowers in Kenya. In Germany, the authorities believe that it is responsible for bird deaths along the Baltic coast.

In addition, there is simply not enough cargo space on airlines flying out of Kenya to handle the trade. Produce has been known to rot at the airports because, though the government has been pushing export agriculture, it has done nothing about providing transport facilities. And poor packaging has begun tilting consumers towards produce from Israeli, South African and Zimbabwean competitors.

On top of this, food items such as cereals are being freed from price control. This will mean that the income from horticulture may no longer be sufficient for farmers to buy food to eat.

Source   Panoscope, April 1994

'Women are also growing flowers on small plots', says Cor van Duyn. 'I don't know why, but when the farms are bigger, they tend to be run by men. On the small shambas it is women who are involved.'

What he doesn't mention is that the prognosis for success for these small plots is not good. But everyone else insists on this.

'Ten years ago, peasants could be involved', says Simon van der Burg, the owner of East African Flowers, a major transporter of Kenyan flowers. 'But now, there's no hope for outgrowing. In Kenya there are a lot of growers going broke. Air freight has gone up. Pricing is very erratic and prices are going to continue to fall. Sulmac is struggling, but it's part of a big multinational. It can absorb losses through the other parts of its business. Small producers can't.'

Flower-growing, say most Kenyan insiders, has to be large-scale because of the costs of marketing, transport and planting materials. It's beyond peasant scope. Propagators of the plants will not sell to smaller growers because of the fear that they will not pay royalties. And the real money is in the new varieties that are in step with fashion among European consumers. USAID and the Kenyan government have programmes to encourage and support small producers, reports say. But the businessmen who know the business insist that these are not going to work in the increasingly competitive climate of today.

Extracts from a speech by David Gray, Sulmac

'Our cold stores at the airport can store 8,000 boxes, and we have our own freighting facilities... With our grading hall we are able to keep more consistency than many of the smaller growers. It does mean that we are producing 3,000 boxes a day, in season, of one quality, and done properly that is a great help to the market.

The market is never satisfied, and if we believed everything our marketing friends told us, we would be in the loony bin. Today they want their lilies open, tomorrow they want them shut; first they want carnations at cut stage four and then at cut stage five... We do quite a lot of overseas trips and we try to keep up to date. We are introducing computerisation...

We do a colour check on all stock that comes in. No variety goes into commercial production until we have seen it for at least 2 years. It is a matter of growing under Kenyan conditions, airfreighting and the time it takes to get to the airport and to get to the market etc...'

Cooperatives of small producers have been set up to try and create critical mass. But a group of them told Van Roozendaal that they were still beset with intractible difficulties. Dutch importers don't take their produce seriously, and they sometimes have water problems, which they cannot solve because of lack of money for irrigation equipment. The roads from their farms are bad and they must depend on middlemen to take their flowers to the airport. Being producers themselves, these middlemen were affected by conflicts of interest between getting their own products to the market and getting those of the outgrowers. Often, they simply didn't show up to collect the produce. Sometimes they would say that the peasants' flowers were rejected by the buyers for quality reasons, and the small farmers would have to take their word for it. Also, they have to accept any price, because they lack independent up-to-date price information.

'Its a game of numbers', explained the marketing manager of one company. 'Its a high-risk business. You have to have the money to take these kinds of risks.'

Environmental effects

'In the next fifty years, there will be no room for production in Europe any more', predicts Cor van Duyn, a pioneer in Kenyan flower-growing. 'There will only be room for clean industry, not for farming'.
Just how dirty the Kenyan production is is difficult to establish for want of studies and investigations. Obviously, those in power would not be interested in having such research done. Thus, according to the scientific evidence available, no significant levels of pesticide residues have yet been found in Lake Naivasha. Many consultants advocating the shift of flower production to Third World countries allege that the high cost of chemical imputs puts a brake on the use of these substances there. All our investigations contradict this. Third World growers must conform to the marketing standards established in the North and the phytosanitary standards for imports into the US and Japan. This implies use of the same production system.

'The same pollution is happening in Africa', observed Martin de Jong, a senior administrator of the Dutch Development Bank, the FMO. 'They're spraying like hell in Africa.'

Pamphil Kweyuh's thorough journalistic effort provides some inklings of the changes that have been taking place in the Kenyan environment as a result of the intensive flower farming, but his findings are difficult to substantiate with scientific evidence. Our suspicions about the long-term effects arise out of the documented effects of the same system in Holland (see relevant chapter).

In addition, all the statements by growers now mention water supply problems and the large plantations have begun to institute drip irrigation systems to conserve water. Most of the farms are located around a large water-source, Lake Naivasha, so the fact that water availability is now becoming a problem may be a reason for alarm. The water table in the lake is definitely sinking but many people say it has done so in the past when there was no flower-farming in the region. According to Chris Maan, a specialist from the Dutch Ministry of Agriculture, there is an additional 15 cm of water being extracted from the lake by the growers every year. He noted in an interview with us that this is likely to rise still further as production is still expanding. In addition, the local population is growing, he pointed out. Thus, water availability in the region is likely to be a problem.

CHAPTER 8

The Case of Zimbabwe
Structural Adjustment and Food Supply

In 1992, a big issue in Zimbabwe was maize banditry. Every week, rural people would hijack trains and make off with sacks of the staple food. They had been turned into criminals by hunger. Drought had hit the southern African country which had once produced so much maize that it had been a net exporter to its neighbours.

Yet, in that same year, Zimbabwe sent 60 million US dollars worth of agricultural produce out of the country, including six million kilograms of water-guzzling flowers, according to its Horticultural Promotion Council. To pay for food imports, the country had to borrow 70 million US dollars from international banks.

'The year 1992 was a most difficult year for Zimbabwe's agricultural industry', observed Dr. R. M. Mupawosa, Chairman of the Agricultural Marketing Authority. 'The levels of crop failure, as a result of the drought, were staggering. The disastrous drought forced us to import food commodities of which we usually have surpluses.'

Nevertheless Zimbabwe was applauded for its economic 'progress' by the international community. It was in the midst of a structural adjustment programme which had dictated that the country switch its orientation towards exports – of products such as flowers, luxury vegetables and fruit. The parastatal companies which had previously handled agricultural produce had been derided as inefficient and forced to get rid of their food surpluses. Restrictions on imports had been dismantled.

To turn Zimbabwe into the model of structural adjustment's success on the African continent, foreign aid donors were pouring masses of money into the country. According to local press reports, 257 million dollars came from the European Community in 1990, followed, in 1991, by a further 300 million dollars through the African Development Bank. Another 700 million dollars came in from assorted donors that year, with Sweden alone promising 28 million for the removal of import controls and Germany 30 million. In 1992, the World Bank, together with the African Development Bank, granted 360 million while the International Monetary Fund started an aid package of 2.45 billion and individual European governments made bilateral contributions – Italy, for example, giving 864 million.

All this was to encourage Zimbabwe to 'divorce socialism and love capitalism' as the International Finance Corporation's regional representative put it. But much of this finance is loan money. The country will have to pay up on its debts – with interest – at some point in the future. Thus, the new export drive must bring high returns on investment.

In the case of flowers, which produces the highest returns of all new agricultural exports, Zimbabwe is one of the Third World's most promising cases. The country has longer experience than most in this field, with a good reputation for exporting quality flowers, up to date with the latest European fashions. Its production jumped by 800 per cent between 1985 and 1990, (from 338 tons to 2,400) and was expected to leap to 6,000 by 1992 (an increase of a further 150 per cent).

Earnings from flowers

Yet, when you look at the returns from this sector in hard currency terms, the results are somewhat disappointing. In 1990, according to local newspapers, flower producers in Zimbabwe were only earning 25 million Zimbabwean dollars (about 5 million US). By 1993, when structural adjustment had nearly halved the value of the local currency, according to the Africa Information Afrique News Service (AIA), the hard currency earnings of flowers was only around 15 million US dollars.

Costs of production

These hard currency earnings should be evaluated against the outflow of money needed to purchase planting material, chemicals, cooling systems, greenhouse equipment, irrigation systems and the expensive services of foreign experts and market specialists. Each hectare of land requires about 400,000 dollars in initial investment before it can produce flowers for export. And then there are the high recurrent costs on chemicals. According to Martin de Jong, Senior Investment Manager for East Africa at the Dutch Development Bank (FMO) which has long been involved in the sector in Zimbabwe, there are 200 hectares under flower cultivation, but the AIA puts the acreage at 550 hectares. We do not have the necessary figures to do the cost-benefit analysis, but it seems clear that it should be done.

Employment consequences

Many foreign advisers say that flower production is good for employment in Third World countries. According to De Jong, 30 people are employed on each hectare that produces flowers in Zimbabwe. There are 300,000 Zimbabweans leaving school each year and looking for work, states Dr Jonathan Moyo, a lecturer in Political and Administrative Studies at the University of Zimbabwe. In total, according to Deutscher Gartenbau, the flower sector employs 3,000 people year-round and 7,000 during its high season and they are paid 165 Zimbabwean dollars per month, which, at current exchange rates, amounts to just over twenty US dollars. Is it wise for so much foreign exchange to be spent in creating such a small proportion of the employment needed? Especially since the success of the sector depends on very low wages and structural adjustment has eliminated subsidies for food and other basic necessities, delegitimised the parastatals' handling of staples and forced the country to go into a 70 million US dollar debt with foreign banks for the importation offood.

Foreign assistance

Money for diversification of agriculture has been coming into Zimbabwe from numerous sources, including, one report states, a 60 million dollar grant from the World Bank. According to Deutscher Gartenbau, the World Bank is also paying for a horticultural research station to be set up.

The pattern of bilateral foreign aid in this sector is well-illustrated by the following example. In 1989, the Dutch government gave Zimbabwe

22 million dollars, specifically to help it buy imports. It is worth noting here that Holland sells Zimbabwe 93 million Zimbabwe dollars worth of goods per year and buys 70 million in Zimbabwean products, including around 80 percent of its flower exports. The following advertisement then appeared in the Zimbabwean press.

Netherlands Commodity Import Programme 1990 (Dfl 20 million)

The Ministry of Trade and Commerce would like to advise the private sector that funds under the above aid programme are now available for disbursement. Interested companies should submit their applications... if they are commercial importers or... industrial importers. Eligible goods under the aid programme must be of either Dutch or developing countries origin and fall under the following categories...

Two things need to be noted here:
1 The aid could only be spent by the private sector, and only by big companies, since only requests of 200,000 Dutch guilders (110,000 US dollars) or more would be entertained.
2 The categories of goods which could be imported with this aid included crop chemicals, plastic raw materials and pump components, all of which are heavily used in the horticulture industry. Developing countries do not produce most of the chemicals and capital goods used by flower-producers. Thus, the money given to Zimbabwe by the Dutch government (i.e. the Dutch taxpayer) as aid would have gone straight back to Dutch industry as payments for imports.

European involvement

Local ownership in the Zimbabwean horticulture industry is largely in the hands of white, former-tobacco farmers. But, according to Deutscher Gartenbau and Zimbabwean newspapers, the country's success in the flower trade is due to the fact that, at an early stage, 'half a dozen Dutch importers managed to expand the range of cut flowers through their own consultancy and cultivation efforts'.

Trade missions have been coming from Holland in the last few years to explore the possible expansion of their involvement in Zimbabwe. This is so important to the two countries that they signed a double taxation agreement in 1990, 'as part of the continuing reform of the local investment climate', as a local newspaper put it.

From Zimbabwe's Financial Gazette, October 20, 1989

'Rose production in Zimbabwe has come a long way since the very first roses were exported from this country in the early 1980s. At that stage there was no technical advice available and no one to advise on what variety of roses should be grown for the export market, with the result that many of the roses that were grown were completely the wrong type, or were already going out of fashion on the European market. The construction of greenhouses, at that stage, was also totally incorrect...

It was not long before the firm W. Kordes' Söhne from West Germany realised the potential and appointed an agent here to represent them in 1989. The firm had been breeding roses for more than a century... Today they are leading breeders of cut-flower roses. This firm has an enterprise in Holland called Interrose... From 1985 new varieties of roses from W. Kordes' Söhne have been coming into the country on an annual basis...

1987 saw a further development in rose production in Zimbabwe with new agencies being given to Cherry Wood's Rose Nursery by De Ruiter's Nieuwe Rozen bv, Holland – leading breeders in the world today of Miniature Roses and Interplant Roses, Holland, the breeders of many of the new Spray Roses which are currently proving to be very popular on the European Markets...

This export season will see the export of cut-blooms of 20 hectares of roses currently being grown by commercial growers in this country and bred by the firm W. Kordes' Söhne. Considerable interest has been shown in Miniature Roses and... this coming season should see an increase to about two and a half hectares...

With the expert advice and assistance by Dutch consultants who are in this country, and with the most up to date varieties of roses available, Zimbabwe can ensure that our product reaching the European markets will be of the very best quality.'

According to Deutscher Gartenbau, among the foreigners supplying the necessary expertise are the large German chemical firms Bayer and Hoechst, the English multinational, ICI, and another company called Windmill.

'Since the political climate has recently turned more friendly to foreign investment, more joint ventures with European companies can be expected', stated the Deutscher Gartenbau.

One European institution which has been involved from the start is the Dutch development bank, the FMO, which is a shareholder in a Zimbabwean flower company. In 1993, the FMO disbursed almost three million US dollars in Zimbabwe's horticulture sector. According to de Jong, the Bank is meant to stimulate private sector investment in Zimbabwe. It gets money from Dutch tax-payers, but is 49 per cent owned by the private sector, which includes large Dutch multinationals such as Philips and Unilever, and is run on strict commercial lines. For instance, says De Jong, the FMO used to give loans for flower-growers elsewhere in Africa, but the bank has now decided that these amounts are too small to make it worthwhile.

'We don't make money on that', he said in an interview.

He himself is on the board of the Zimbabwe Development Bank, which receives money from the FMO, and he is uneasy about the ZDB's funding of too many new flower businesses in the country. There is big competition from abroad, he feels. The sector should be consolidated instead of just being allowed to spread wildly, since he believes that already about a quarter of the flower farms in Zimbabwe are making a loss. Local people should be trained to take over a greater share of the technical areas of production.

'This business must be sectorally developed', he says. 'You have to have the political lobbies such as the farming lobbies here in Europe. We are willing to put money into a training institute.'

The intractable problem of air transportation

In trying to encourage this sectoral development, the FMO has co-financed a feasibility study by the Horticultural Producers Council to set up a private airline. For Zimbabwe, one of the pioneers of Third World flower production, has fully demonstrated the vulnerability of this delicate trade to the whims of the air-transportation business. Producers in this distant land can only depend on their national airline, Affretair, to transport their product. The airline has difficulties in doing this, since there is little air-freight to be brought in the other direction. Between 1987 and 1990, its freight costs have doubled, reducing the profit margins dramatically for the producers. This causes a constant stream of two-way vituperation in the Zimbabwean press between the airline and the producers. In 1990, according to the Deutscher Gartenbau, one million flowers remained in Harare because of problems with Affretair. Affretair keeps hoping that other airlines will step in and take up the slack.

Then, in 1989, the vulnerability at the heart of the flower business exploded in the Zimbabwean press. Zimbabwe raised landing rights costs for KLM, the Dutch national carrier and Holland responded by refusing Affretair landing rights at Amsterdam's Schiphol airport. Millions of dollars in export earnings were lost as a result. The flowers had to be routed through Germany and then trucked back to the flower market in Holland, losing time, freshness and price.

The workers' point of view

The incident demonstrated the vulnerability of a weak country which is economically dependent on this commodity. But there are other negative consequences which are not being documented. The following article from the Africa Information Afrique news service presents the flower trade as seen by workers.

'Boss thinks flowers are more important than people'

Harare, Zimbabwe, March 25, 1993 – Last year, Leave Ndlovu's life mysteriously began to fall to pieces.

His wife and workmates at a horticultural farm near Harare noticed that the thirty-year-old pesticide mixer was developing strange behaviour. Ndlovu's eyes ran incessantly, he complained of debilitating dizziness, nausea and disorientation, and his speech became slurred to the point of incoherence.

In October he spent two weeks in hospital, where doctors puzzled over his symptoms. Only after he was retrenched was the cause of his illness, chronic pesticide poisoning, properly diagnosed. Ndlovu, unemployed, ailing and divorced, is now waiting at his village home for the results of a union-led action for a disability pension from his former employer.

According to Sammy Chaikosa, the health and safety officer of the General Agricultural and Plantation Workers' Union of Zimbabwe, Ndlovu is part of the first wave of victims of occupational hazards in the young horticultural industry. Many others suffer in silence.

Since its quiet beginnings in 1985, the Zimbabwean cut flower industry has expanded rapidly to become a multi-million dollar export business involving more than 450 farms. In the last two years horticulture – including fine vegetables, herbs, essential oils, citrus and other fruits – has been the fastest growing sector in Zimbabwe... This year flower exports are expected to top 151,200,000 Zimbabwe dollars (roughly 19 million US dollars), half of that earned in sales of roses.

In the new era of structural adjustment, government looks favourably on the industry and has diverted substantial amounts of foreign currency into the sector. Farmers say a good chunk of that money goes towards importing a wide range of pesticides, fungicides and fertilizers essential to the industry's highly capital-intensive production. Some of the chemicals are extremely toxic.

Farmers and their co-ordinating body, the Horticulture Promotion Council (HPC), claim that access to and use of dangerous chemicals is strictly controlled and monitored... Yet some of these restrictions are regularly broken at many horticultural operations. At one farm outside Harare, workers complain that they are forced to work without gloves, wearing threadbare overalls or their own clothes. While those workers designated to apply chemicals are provided with protective gear, pruners and other greenhouse workers go without.

'The sprayers come through while we are working', says a man with badly scarred hands. 'We can smell those chemicals. We know that is bad for us. Many suffer from headaches and sore eyes. My hands get pricked, and those chemicals get into my body. But if you complain, you have no job. Complainers get fired.'

In September, a fellow pruner, 24-year-old Grey Chimosva, was working without gloves, goggles or mask when granules of the highly-toxic pesticide Temic got into his eyes.

'My sight went black and my eyes ran with water. The boss took me to the hospital, where I was treated for two days. The boss told me to tell the doctor that I had been in full combat gear and that the wind blew the dust into my eyes.

'When I went back to the farm I still couldn't see right. I went to a nearby clinic for three days, but that didn't help. Now (the boss) says that if I don't work, there is no job. But my eyes still hurt, and I cannot see anything unless it is near to me.'

The HPC and individual farmers claim that those handling chemicals are given full instruction about their dangers, and that other workers are also educated about the hazards of greenhouse substances.

'Permanent and casual labourers are both given training and educational materials. The horticultural industry emphasizes human safety', says the HPC's Stanley Neri. 'Officials for the ministry of labour's Occupational Health and Safety section make sure to visit every horticultural farm at least once a year, giving talk and showing films.'

Yet farm workers interviewed said they had never seen or heard of any visitors from the ministry. Farmers, too, testified that their operations had never been inspected or investigated by government officials.

'The HPC's talking nonsense', says GAPWUZ's Chaikosa.

'I was sent to a course for training about chemicals', a foreman recounts. 'The course was supposed to last ten days. I went for one day only. The boss said there was more important work on the farm, that I was needed. At the course they told us that only a few of the chemicals were really dangerous. Me – I don't believe it. But the boss said I had to tell the sprayers what I had learned, so I did.'

'Boss thinks flowers are more important than people', said a pruner. 'We would like good overalls, masks, boots and gloves. We would like better water and housing. he says there is no money. But he's still expanding – four hectares of greenhouses, that's millions. He makes money and that's where it goes.'

GAPWUZ anticipates that more cases of chronic and acute poisoning arising from slack standards in horticulture will become common as the industry expands, and more workers are exposed to risks in the long term. Horticultural producers are enlarging their operations with government encouragement in an effort to cash in on lucrative markets five thousand miles to the North. This season, more than 550 hectares of flowers are in production.

Source   Africa Information Afrique

Other foreseeable consequences

1 Food Supply: The 1992 food crisis made plain the vulnerability of Zimbabwe's food security. The country is prone to drought – it had one just five years before the 1992 catastrophe. It is clear that for future disasters to be averted, provisions should be made with respect to food supplies. But at present the focus is on export agriculture instead.

2 Much of the money that is flowing into Zimbabwe to help it change its economic policy is in the form of loans. These will have to be paid back in the future. If the 'high-value' export crops such as flowers do not bring in the net foreign-exchange earnings that are expected, the country will end up with a huge debt that it will be unable to pay.

CHAPTER 9

The Case of India
Joint Ventures and Tax Exemptions

'It's all tax-driven', observed Jan Lanning of the Dutch Wholesale Board in describing India's aggressive attempts in the early nineties to leap into the international flower-market. India's large industrialists, he suggested, are merely trying to get access to the substantial tax exemptions offered by the government for developing export-crops in the era of structural adjustment and debt.

However, they alone are not responsible for this. Dutch companies are frantically setting up joint ventures with the Indians, believing that the lucrative flower-trade in Asia can be extended into an export-oriented one through a certain degree of modernisation. However, as local commentators note, the local market is for 'low-quality' flowers, as most are used in rituals of worship. Consumers do not demand beauty, durability or novelty when they purchase a garland. The traditional gods are not so fussy. The European consumer, on the other hand, is. And her aesthetic orientation is vastly different. So there is a huge learning process that must take place in India before the country becomes competitive in the international sector. Moreover, India does not get the tariff exemptions of African and Latin American countries in relation to the EU market. Levies of 15-20 per cent have to be taken account of in attaining profitability.

Thus, it is possibly going to be some time before India becomes a serious player in the flower business. But when it does, the effects are likely to be profound because of the large-scale initiatives taking place there.

Since the case of India illustrates very well the latest global dynamics in this industry, we have chosen to reproduce here large extracts from a report written by Bharad Dogra of New Delhi. It points to the kinds of joint ventures that are taking place between foreign and local firms in this area, the facilitating mechanisms governments are establishing and the role of international development organisations. In all the Indian cases cited, buy-back arrangements are mentioned; that is, the foreign partners in the joint ventures are expected to supply technology and buy the resulting produce via their Europe-based marketing and distribution companies.

Extracts from 'Emerging Trends in Floriculture'[46]

There have been several indications in recent months that floriculture is fast emerging as an important area of growth in Indian agriculture and agribusiness. In particular, export-oriented floriculture appears to be heading for a boom time. A number of corporations from India as well as forign countries (...) have evinced keen interest and signed collaboration agreements. The government appears to be fully backing these efforts in the form of sending and hosting trade delegations, removing restrictions on the imports of seeds and equipment, making quarantine clearances easier and quicker than before and of course, providing a number of incentives and concessions for increasing the exports of flowers (...)

The Observer [a local newspaper] reported:
    'India is poised to get the much-cherished foothold in the international cut flower market with a consortium of local private and public sector companies and foreign firms entering an agreement to set up 100 per cent export-oriented units in the country. This will also mark the entry of the Metal and Minerals Trading Corporation (MMTC) into export-oriented floriculture industry in a big way. The participants in the joint venture in floriculture include Filiclair of France, Kurd Consultancy Services of India, Ofman Verbeek International BV and Geerlofs Refrigeration BV of Holland. All these foreign companies are well known in international floriculture circles. They formed a consortium at the initiative of Kurd Consultancy Services of India which has considerable experience in developing floriculture as an export-oriented industry in the Third World (...)
    'Estimated to cost Rs. 20 crore [one crore equals ten million], the joint venture will have a 40-acre farm having greenhouses, precooling house, drip irrigation etc. The annual turnover is expected to be about 21

crore rupees of which about 18.5 would be in foreign exchange. The annual production is estimated at about 7.2 million roses, 15 million carnations and about 8 million chrysanthemums. It would employ about 500 persons, mostly women. The consortium members will not only transer the relevant technology but would also buy back the products. About 35 per cent foreign equity participation is envisaged. The managers will be trained in Holland and France.

'The other Indian joint venture having similar agreement terms is Biotech International Ltd (...) The latest initiative made by this consortium is the setting up of a 100 per cent export-oriented joint sector floriculture unit in Nepal. This venture is likely to get assistance from the EEC. The participating Nepalese company is Agriflora Pvt Ltd, a subsidiary of Vaidya group of companies. The consortium has offered equity, technology transer, buy-back and essential infrastructure and raw materials (...) This consortium now proposes to have a joint venture in India for exploiting the floriculture potential of north-eastern states.'

The Economic Times reported in 1994:

'The Sohna-based Karishma Floriculture Ltd (KFL), a 100 per cent export-oriented Indo-Dutch project, is all set for commercial production. KFL's Dutch collaborator, Dalsem BV of the Van Dijk Holding Group, has technically okayed the captive 'cold chain' developed by the Indian collaborator (...) which is meant to rush the consignment of fresh flowers to the IGIA, situated 30 kms from the KFL's greenhouses. Mr Bansal told the Economic Times that 'during their visit to India in February, the Dutch floriculture Mission led by Mr Van der Schaft, external relations director of the Netherland Development Finance Corporation, Dalsem of Holland, had signed a memorandum of understanding with KFL, on the persuasion of Mr Gokul Patnaik, chairman, Agricultural and Processed Food Products Exports Development Authority (APEDA). The entire product of the KFL's Sohna unit is under buy-back arrangement with the Dutch collaborator (...).'

The Tribune reported in 1994:

'Oriental Flowers, a Tata group company set up in 1991, exports to West Asia and Europe, while a newly established Harrison Universal Flowers Ltd, set up in collaboration with French principals Universal Flowers Ltd, produces patented French-variety roses, for export to

France and the Ruja's Essar Agrotech, with technical collaboration with Dutch assistance, sells to the Amsterdam market.

'There are about 30 to 40 proposals pending, waiting for sanction from us for setting up floriculture units in different parts of the country', says Gokul Patnaik, chairman of APEDA.'

The Business India reported recently (March 1994):

'Sensing an enormous opportunity here, a Dutch delegation visited India recently to hawk its expertise – technology, greenhouses, et al. Besides, India also has the potential for being a lucrative market for exporting plantlets too. As Canada-based Prairie Plant System Inc, a biotechnology research and development company discovered. It has signed a Memorandum of Understanding with Baramati Agro to develop tissue culture operations in India. Says Vice-President, Cary Storey, India can act as a very effective nursery – owing to low labour costs and favourable conditions.'

Earlier the same magazine reported on some other projects:

'According to Gurumurthy Narajan, a US-trained agronomist who is now general manager with Essar Agrotech, the project involved 4 hectares of polyhouses growing 320,000 roseplants near Pune. All the plants are imported from the Netherlands and would give an average yield of about 180 to 200 stems per square metre, he said. The project, including the polyhouses, highly sophisticated irrigation systems, precooling facilities, administration and other infrastructure would cost about 5.5 crores of rupees. The company has a tie-up with Moerheim roses of Holland for a technical and marketing collaboration.

'Another rose cultivation project being funded by the ACE programme has been conceived by Deccan Florabase Ltd. According to Bimal Shroff, director of the company, the project envisages building of the largest poly-house in the country, spread over 4.5 hectares at Vagdam Maval, also near Pune. Shroff has also tied up with Flodac BV, another Dutch company, for a technical and buy-back arrangement. The project, which will cost about 8 crores of rupees, envisages exports of over 9.5 million rose stems a year.'

The National Herald reported on February 10, 1994 on the government's efforts in this direction:

'The Commerce Ministry has identified floriculture as an extreme focus segment to boost exports to 100 crores of rupees by 1996-7, despite imposition of stiff tariffs ranging from 15-20 per cent by European nations at the conclusion of the GATT negotiations. The euphoria over flower exports was borne out by the fact that nearly 50,000 hectares in the country had already been brought under floriculture to serve the vast domestic market and for exports to emerging markets in the Asia-Pacific region.

'According to APEDA chairman, Gokul Patnaik, seven projects of an average three hectares each had been identified to set up high technology greenhouses to bring Indian growers at par with their competitors, mainly Kenya and Colombia. He said a number of positive changes had taken place after submission of a report by an expert group in 1992. The import duty on all goods falling within Chapter six of the first schedule of the customs tariff Act 1975 was reduced from 55 per cent to 10 per cent. These included live trees and other plants, bulbs, roots and the like, cut flowers and ornamental foliage. The seeds tubers, bulb cuttings or saplings for sowing and planting were exempted from customs duty.

'Plant quarantine procedures had been streamlined and simplified to a considerable extent to provide expeditious clearance to the import of seeds, plants, tubers and cuttings. Tissue cultures now get cleared within six hours and other consignments requiring quarantine within two days. The import of flower seeds and tissue culture material of any plant origin was now being allowed without the need of an import permit.'

In this context, it is interesting that a United Nations Development Programme-aided project has been recently launched in India in the area of floriculture which promises to provide advice on eco-friendly pest control methods and achievement of international quality standards through minimum use of chemicals. This project will provide grants worth 19 Million rupees over three years to assist a significant expansion of India's cut flower exports.

CHAPTER 10

The Case of the Netherlands
Trouble in the Centre

Environmental damage, unhealthy working conditions and bad social policy accompany flower growing wherever one looks, and not only in the Third World. Also in the Netherlands, the world's main flower power *and* a wealthy industrialized country, profits are made at the expense of land and labour.[47]

Some figures on Dutch floriculture first. In 1993, total production value was 5.9 billion guilders (3.7 billion dollars), up from 4.9 billion in 1989. Roughly two thirds can be attributed to cut flowers. Exports amounted to 4.9 billion guilders (2.8 billion dollars). In 1990 it was calculated that the flowers and plants sector contributed 0.71 per cent to the country's GDP. Cut flowers can be estimated to make up just under 0.5 per cent of GDP.

Economically speaking, the industry is doing quite well. According to Jan Ruhé, who has experience in practically any segment of the Dutch cut flower industry, breeders and propagators are doing fine, as is shown by their current capacity for investment. Wholesale and retail trade have no reason for complaint, even though computerised price information systems have made the business predictable, and therefore boring to some people's taste. Most exposed to risk are the growers, Ruhé says. When the economic path somehow turns bumpy, they get most of the bruises.

But figures of the Dutch Agricultural Economic Institute[48] (LEI) show that even growers have been able to cope with changing conditions. Their net result was 95 per cent or more in six out of ten years between 1983 and 1992. In the other four years it was between 90 and 94 per cent.

According to Magda de Vetten of the Commodity Board for Floricultural Products, a result of 95 per cent is 'fairly good', whereas 93 per cent is 'unsatisfactory'.[*]

Pesticides

In Dutch floriculture, as elsewhere, pesticides are major pollutants. Spraying (or fogging, a more advanced technique) is intensive at all stages of production. Before planting, the soil is disinfected. During growth, diseases and pests, fungi, insects and harmful soil organisms are controlled *preventively*, i.e. without regard to whether these problems are really occurring. Also, hormone-like substances accelerating or retarding plant growth are applied to make the flowers harvest-ready at the desired moment. After cutting, the flowers are treated with bacteria-killers in order to make them last and look fresh longer.

The use of these chemicals varies strongly from one sort of flower to the next and from one grower to the next. Lilies are notorious pesticide junkies, demanding nearly 250 kilos of active ingredients per hectare per year. Irises, narcissi and tulips consume between 100 and 200 kilos. Alstroemerias, gerberas, freesias, carnations, chrysanthemums and roses survive on 25-75 kilos. As to the variety among growers, the more environmentally conscious ones have managed to halve pesticide use from 80 to 40 kilos in chrysanthemums by switching from preventive to curative spraying.[**]

All growers are having to make a similar effort, since the entire agricultural sector has through an official agreement with the national

---

[*]   Technically, the break-even point lies at 100 percent. The method of calculation, however, assumes a unrealistically high income level for the flower grower and his/her family members. A result of 95 percent implies a somewhat lower income, not a disastrous loss. A result of 76 percent, as fruit growers recently achieved, does.

[**]   Given these figures, it is hilarious to find a rose grower quoted by the Parool daily as saying, 'we have to deal with high environmental standards, [whereas] in Africa, they *do* use toxic substances.'

government committed itself to reduce pesticide use by 35 per cent by 1996 as compared to the period 1984-1988. The Commodity Board for Floricultural Products claims the sector it represents is ahead of schedule.

Both the water and the air of the flower-growing regions, situated in the West of the country, are severely contaminated. Of all poisonous 'leakages' 90 per cent is to the atmosphere. Part of these emissions lands in the direct surroundings. Dry and wet precipitations (dust and rain) contain high amounts of pesticides. These airborne toxic particles are a particular health hazard to people living right next to the greenhouses, often just at a few metres' distance. No health survey has taken place so far among this risk-group.

The other groups at risk are, obviously, the workers in the greenhouses (some 30,000 people) and, more surprisingly, florists (22,500 people[49] – flower shops in the Netherlands even outnumber bicycle repair shops). The workers are exposed to concentrations of up to 60 times the concentration considered to be safe, according to a study of highly regarded experts, published by the country's Ministry of Social Affairs and Employment.[50] Depending on the type of pesticide, concentrations in the air at the moment of the workers' reentry into the greenhouse are still between 200 and 1200 micrograms per cubic metre ($\mu g/m^3$), whereas the study puts the acceptable level at 20 $\mu g/m^3$. The acceptable level can be attained by ventilating the greenhouse for at least two hours – which, in turn, worsens the emissions to the outside world. Several of the pesticides used, such as chlorothalonil, etridiazole, zineb, dichloropropene, propoxur and thiophanate-methyl have been conclusively proven to cause cancer in test animals, while many others are suspected of doing so.

Florists come into this story because of the second main route through which pesticides enter the human body: through the skin. The concentrations to which they are exposed while handling the flowers are for some chemicals (dimethoate, benomyl, methamidophos, chlorothalonil) above the safety thresholds established on the basis of animal tests. Greenhouse workers' also run this additional risk. Even consumers who put the flowers into the vase may have reason to dread the residues of the pesticide cocktails. 'We are getting signals from consumers' organizations, for instance in Switzerland, that they want to look into this', Hans Muilerman of the Zuidhollandse Milieufederatie says.

Of the toxic emissions, 10 per cent goes to the ground and surface water. Since the seventies, the ground water in the flower growing regions has been deemed unsuitable for conversion into drinking water – in a country that manages to confer tap quality to Rhine water contaminated by a joint effort of the chemical companies Sandoz in Switzerland, Hoechst and BASF in Germany and salt mines in France. The ground water is expected to remain unsuitable for several generation.

As for ditches and canals in the flower-growing regions, quite a few of them are 'ecologically dead'. Only the hardiest species, a few worms and snails in particular, eke out a living in this inhospitable milieu. To less macho characters, such as water flees, the water is poisonous even after hundredfold dilution. In some water samples, concentrations of toxic substances (dichlorovos, parathion) exceeding the maximum concentration allowed by several thousand times were detected. In the case of one chemical, a concentration of over 60,000 times the maximum value was found.

Energy

Dutch flower growing, especially in winter, is very energy-intensive. The extremely high yields per hectare that Dutch growers attain require large amounts of fertilizer, which in the Netherlands is inexpensive (only 2 per cent of production costs) thanks mainly to the low energy prices charged to domestic chemical industry. Horticulturalists are charged equally low prices (12 US¢ per cubic metre, about half the price households pay), which the energy authorities can offer thanks to the enormous natural-gas reserves the country boasts. Since it is to a large extent the low energy price that has kept Dutch flower (and vegetable) growers competitive, it is often said that what they export is not so much roses and tomatoes, but gas in a different shape.

The other side of this coin are the substantial emissions of carbon dioxide associated with the sector. In 1991, direct emissions amounted to 2.9 million tons of CO_2, up from 1.8 million tons six years earlier.[51] Already this is over 1.5 per cent of total Dutch emissions (185 million tons), and it does not even include the emissions caused by energy use for fertilizer production and flower transport.

Labour

Horticulture (especially bulb production, but also other subsectors) is the second biggest employer of illegal labour in the Netherlands, that is labour without a proper contract. Many of these workers are illegal in a double sense: they also lack the required residence permit, which puts them completely at their employers' mercy. The latter benefit in many ways: social security contributions are nil, wages are very low for local standards, job security is non-existent. The phenomenon of illegal labour in horticulture and other sectors is sometimes dubbed 'the Third World creeping into the First World'. The pitiable housing conditions of many of these illegal workers provides additional food to the metaphor.

The Netherlands Economic Institute[52] estimates that up to 21 per cent of all labour in horticulture is done by illegal workers: 8,500 man-years out of a total of 40,000. One out of three horticultural companies employs some illegal labour. Only in tailoring establishments is this proportion thought to be higher (43 per cent of all labour); and only in the hotel and catering sector is the total amount of illegal labour larger (9,600 man-years). Unlike the latter two, horticultural employers claim they resort to this illicit practice for want of Dutch unemployed willing to do these jobs. The reason for this unwillingness is the low wage paid for the hard and unhealthy work.

CHAPTER 11

Conclusions

'Would *you* invest in flowers in some Third World country?' we asked
one consultant.

'If you compare it to all other agricultural commodities, I would go
for flowers', he answered.

We wouldn't. Not if we were Third World policy-makers; not if we
were Third World investors.

On the surface, the picture for the Third World looks bright:
booming exports, moaning Dutch competitors, high returns on capital,
enthusiasm throughout the world of development finance. There is
enough encouragement around to trigger off investors' killing instincts.

'You can make a calculation on the back of an envelope to show that
growing flowers is tremendously lucrative', one source told us.

A look beyond the consultants' claims, however, shows the cracks in
the shiny façade.

First, there are the purely economic doubts about profitability
prospects and benefits to the country involved. Even now, many
companies are not doing well. In Zimbabwe, a quarter of them are
running at a loss, according to Martin de Jong of the Dutch
development bank. Similar problems are said to exist in Kenya; even
giant Sulmac is widely reputed to be in difficulties. Flower growing is
notorious for the multiple risks that lurk at every corner, ranging from
weather vicissitudes to air transport capriciousness to consumer whim.

More importantly, general profitability prospects are dubious, to say
the least. Supply, especially to the crucial European market, has been
skyrocketing and shows no sign of levelling off. As more countries
engage in the same venture, supply will grow even further. Colombia is
shifting its flow towards Europe, there is a rose rush going on in African
countries, and India might get its act together and terminally flood the
market.

While increasing smoothly, demand is unlikely to keep up with this
bloom boom. Whether or not India becomes a major party, prices for

roses seem set to decline, following the example of carnations and alstroemerias. And, of course, of cocoa, tea, coffee, sisal, jute and groundnuts before those.

The resulting squeeze on profits could theoretically be offset by moving into more securely rewarding segments of the flower sector: breeding, propagating, growing high-value varieties, transport, trading. But the Northern players seem determined *and* well-placed to cling to these geese with their golden eggs. They are near to the market and have technological advantages that they are enhancing year by year.

Even when a flower growing company makes good profits, what benefits accrue to the Third World country where it happens to be based? Of course, there are some wages paid, but these are at the lowest level. Governments can charge fees for export licences and levy taxes on profits. But all over Africa, extensive tax holidays are becoming standard practice. In Peru, the generous profits of Peter Ullrich, who pioneered floriculture in the country, were not taxed from 1982 to 1991.[53]

Moreover, there is immense scope for manipulation of business figures in this fast-paced and little-controlled sector, so that tax evasion is an easy matter. According to our sources, Brooke Bond's (Unilever's) aim in buying Sulmac was not so much to become a player in floriculture but to sluice profits made in Kenya to Europe.

The reason cited by development economists, consultants and creditor banks for taking to flowers in the first place is hard-currency earnings. But a calculation of the net dollar flow to the state, after subtracting expenses, might well make for a disconcerting figure.

At a more general level of economic analysis, there are other negative structural effects of the flower business. There is hardly any room at all for small farmers, who lack capital, timely information about demand and credibility in breeders' eyes. Even large local farmers often do not get a foothold. In Latin America and India, it is mainly non-agrarian entrepreneurs extending their business into a new sector; in Kenya and Zimbabwe, most company owners are either foreigners or belong to the white elite. Only 3 per cent of company owners are black Kenyans. This distorts possibilities of development of the agrarian sector and has profound implications for long-term social and economic development in general. It shifts the focus in training and research away from sectors that are more likely to contribute to coherent rural development, and promotes the notion that a dignified independent rural livelihood is an unachievable goal.

Also, food production tends to suffer. In the Bogotá savannah, foodstuffs have become dear because they have to be brought in from other parts of the country. Higher food prices were also observed in Peru's flower centre, the Huaylas Valley and in Kenya. In Zimbabwe, the economic policy that emphasized growing export crops like flowers led to nation-wide scarcity in the staple food, maize, in 1992.

Furthermore, the Third World flower sector, with its breath-taking speed, glossy modern image and high competitiveness, seems to encourage a culture of rapaciousness in the rural environment. In Colombia, flower growers are among the most ruthless employers, not to mention their suspected links with drugs. In Kenya, according to many of our sources, several very top people in the country's corrupt regime have got involved. These facts do not spell any good for either the workers or the state coffers.

Secondly, there are the things most macro-economists would overlook as external costs, or side-effects to be remedied through good governance – except that they *are* not remedied, and do take their toll. We mean the social and environmental problems that seem to accompany flower growing.

To be fair, some flower companies do treat their workers properly, paying them fair wages, building in health considerations, and allowing them to organize themselves in accordance with international standards. Unfortunately, these companies are untypical. Keeping wages as low as possible is the favoured method, in both North and South, of facing down the competition in this sector. Hiring workers from vulnerable groups, unlikely to get silly ideas about trade unions into their heads, helps to do that. In Holland, this means hiring illegal immigrants. In Latin America, uneducated peasant women fulfil the same purpose. In Africa, the plantation structure set in the old colonial days, including the relationships of personal dependence which come with that, does the trick.

As to the ecological side, apart from the odd, very marginal organic grower, commercial flowers invariably spell trouble.

Pesticides are used in most crops, of course, and carelessly most of the time. However, in flowers they are particularly intensively applied. This can easily contaminate surface and ground water – the Dutch experience is clear. When used in the closed greenhouse environment, they are particularly dangerous to the workers. How dangerous, is well illustrated by the experiences of the Colombian flower workers. But also in Africa, there is a shift going on from open-air growing to greenhouse production in order to meet quality standards, so that the typical problems will spread there as well.

Flowers cannot be grown without an abundant supply of water – a scarce resource in many places. In Colombia, rivers have shrunk to little streams and the ground water table has fallen by tens of metres. In Kenya, around Lake Naivasha, the growers are worrying that the falling of the water table may be more than just an incident. This has important implications for human health and the possibilities for other agricultural production.

Air transport to the Northern markets consumes tremendous amounts of jet fuel. This may not harm the local environment, but it does add to the risks of climate change. Air transport is also strongly suspected of damaging the ozone layer. This problem is unlikely to affect the tropics very much, but may cause havoc in the temperate regions.

So, if the workers and the environment suffer, prospects for profit in the medium term are dubious, the national economy does not benefit much, local (African) business, except for a small elite, gets a very slim portion of the pie, food security is put at risk and traditional inequalities in societies are deepened, why should any Third World country go for flowers?

The answer lies in the assumptions underpinning our consultant's statement.

'If you compare it to all other agricultural commodities, I would go for flowers', he had said.

He is perfectly right that flowers are, right now and as long as it lasts, the most profitable of agricultural commodities. *Given* the insistence on exports by conventional economic wisdom, and *given* the compulsion to pay back a debt incurred long ago, and *given* the low prices for traditional agricultural export crops; given these multiple pressures, it is hard to avoid the conclusion that the only path to redemption is through the rose-garden.

But if the best you can get as long as you respect these givens is floriculture, with all its flaws and risks and thorny sides, you begin to wonder if these very givens shouldn't be, well – given back.

Perhaps that will create room for thought about real economic solutions that put people's needs first and that include the long-term economic, social and ecological perspective. Sustainable development, in other words. For once you start questioning flower growing, you end up questioning the development model that prepared the ground for it.

Notes

1   Estimate on the basis of Joy Pakenham-Walsh, *Floricultural Products. A survey of the Netherlands and other major markets in the European Community*, CBI, Rotterdam, 1993, p. 18, and *Yearbook 1993*, AIPH, p. 84 and 163.

2   L.W. Waithaka, *The horticultural industry in Kenya*, lecture presented at HORTEC '94 seminar in Nairobi, March 1994.

3   Isebill V. Gruhn, *'Say it with flowers'*, University of California, Santa Cruz, 1991; p. 15.

4   'Thailands Handel mit Orchideen blüht', in: *Nachrichten für den Aussenhandel*, 3 March 1992.

5   Cees van Vliet, 'Als thee het er goed doet, doen bloemen het er zeker', in: *Vakblad voor de bloemisterij*, 1994, 23, p. 48-51.

6   Cees van Vliet, Beeld in Nederland van Afrikaan is vol vooroordelen, in: *Vakblad voor de Bloemisterij*, 1994, 27, p. 24-29.

7   Cees van Vliet, Beeld in Nederland van Afrikaan is vol vooroordelen, in: *Vakblad voor de Bloemisterij*, 1994, 27, p. 29.

8   Bonarius, 'Say it with flowers', in: *Courier*, March/April 1994, p. 4-5.

9   Lecture entitled 'Global Scenario for Floriculture 2000', by ir. ing. Herman de Boon, Cebeco Handelsraad Group, Rotterdam. Source unknown.

10 M. Haak, H. Tap and A.M.A. Heybroek, *A view of International competitiveness in the Florestry Industry*, Rabobank, Eindhoven, 1992, p. 8.

11 Pakenham-Walsh, p. 17.

12 Vakblad voor de Bloemisterij, 1994, issue 4.

13 Vakblad voor de Bloemisterij, 1994, issue 27, p. 25.

14 The Herald (Harare), 2 April 1992.

15 Vakblad voor de Bloemisterij, issue 4, 1994.

16 M. Haak *et.al.*, p. 5.

17 *Vakblad voor de Bloemisterij*, 1994, 27, p. 26.

18 *Nachrichten für den Aussenhandel*, 3 March 1992.

19   *Vakblad voor de Bloemisterij,* 1994, 25, p. 51.
20   Some good information on air freight in Edward Bent, Kein Platz
     für Blumen in der Luft? In: *Deutscher Gartenbau,* 1992, p. 1377-1379.
21   Piet van Seeters, 'Importbloem krijgt last van milieukeur', in: *de*
     Volkskrant, 27 July 1994.
22   Sarah Stewart, *Colombian flowers: the gift of love and poison,* page 7,
     Christian Aid, 1994.
23   Stewart, p. 7.
24   Karin Albers, 'Geen rozen zonder doornen', in *Onze Wereld,* April
     1993, p. 61.
25   *Blumenrundbrief* Nr. 13, p. 7, FIAN, Herne, 1993.
26   Bettina Reiss, 'Sie rauben uns nicht nur unsere Arbeitskraft, sondern
     auch die Liebe unserer Kinder', in: Frank Brassel and Ralf Piorr,
     Blütenträume – Wirtschaftsmacht, p. 20, DGB-Bildungswerk e.V.,
     Nord-Süd-Netz, Düsseldorf, 1992.
27   Reiss, p. 19.
28   Stewart, p. 8.
29   Reiss, p. 22. Health problems mentioned in Reiss and Stewart.
30   Frank Brassel and Ralf Piorr, 'Blühende Träume – verwelktes
     Erwachen', p. 37, in: same authors, *Blütenträume, Wirtschaftsmacht.*
31   Verena Meier, *Frische Blumen aus Kolumbien,* p. 109/110, Basel, 1993.
32   FIAN, 'The situation of the flower workers in Colombia', p. 18, in:
     Hungry for what is right, 1994.
33   Meier, p. 110.
34   FIAN, 'The situation of the flower workers in Colombia', p. 19.
35   Stewart, p. 4.
36   Meier, p. 111.
37   *Blumenrundbrief* Nr. 8, p. 5, FIAN, 1992
38   Stewart, p. 5.
39   Stewart, p. 6.
40   Information on water: *Blumenrundbrief* Nr. 10 and 13; Reiss, p. 22;
     Albers, p. 60; Stewart, p. 5-6.
41   Stewart, p. 7. According to Reiss, in nearly 20 percent of companies
     there is a union.
42   *Blumenrundbrief* Nr. 14.
43   AIPH Yearbook of the International Horticultural Statistics, 1993, p.
     84 and 163.
44   Stewart, p. 9.

45 Stewart, p. 9-10 and 7.
46 Bharat Dogra, *Emerging Trends in Floriculture*, New Delhi, 1994.
47 A regional environmental organization, the Zuidhollandse Milieufederatie, has been dogging the sector since about 1989, collecting available data and publicizing them. Their specialist is Hans Muilerman, who is also the main author of *Snijbloementeelt en milieu* (Zuidhollandse Milieufederatie, Rotterdam, 1994), on which this chapter draws heavily.
48 Quoted in *Kwantitatieve informatie voor de glastuinbouw, 1993-1994*, Informatie en Kennis Centrum Akker- en Tuinbouw, afdeling glasgroente en bloemisterij, Aalsmeer/Naaldwijk 1993.
49 According to the Flower Council of Holland in Leiden.
50 D.H. Brouwer and J.A.F. de Vreede, *Het verdwijnen van bestrijdingsmiddelen uit kaslucht na toepassing met een laag-volumetechniek*, Ministerie van Sociale Zaken en Werkgelegenheid, The Hague, 1992.
51 *Energie in de glastuinbouw van Nederland in 1991*, Landbouweconomisch Instituut and NOVEM, The Hague, 1992.
52 Quoted by the *Agrarisch Dagblad* (Agrarian Daily), 21 October 1993, p. 1 and 3.
53 Luis Gomero Osorio, Walter Chamochumbi Chávez and Kees van den Burg, *Las flores, ¿un callejón sin salida?*, Red de Acción en Alternativas al Uso de Agroquímicas, Lima, 1992, p. 46.